"AMONG THOSE WHO DISLIKE OPPRESSION
ARE MANY WHO LIKE TO OPPRESS"
– NAPOLEON

©2023 CATHERINE FET · NORTH LANDING BOOKS · ALL RIGHTS RESERVED

HOW IT ALL STARTED

The Age of Revolutions in Europe opened with the French Revolution of 1789 and lasted until the late 19th century, rumbling through 2 more revolutions in France (1830, 1848) as well as numerous uprisings and wars of independence across Europe. In this book we'll explore the early decades of this turbulent era – from the French Revolution through the Napoleonic Era.

The French Revolution is associated with dramatic scenes, such as the storming of the Bastille prison and the execution of the French King Louis XVI and Queen Marie Antoinette. Its roots, however, run deep into European and American history. The first royal head to roll was that of King Charles I during the English Civil War, in 1649.

In 1215, facing a rebellion of his barons (land owning noblemen), England's King John (the evil King John of the Robin Hood legends!) agreed to a charter of rights, the **Magna Carta** (the 'Great Charter' in Latin). It established a council of barons to serve as the king's advisors. The council was soon named the **Parliament**. The Parliament became an elected body, divided into the **House of Commons** and the **House of Lords**, and its authority grew until the reign of King Charles I in the 17th century.

"King John agrees to sign the Magna Carta" by Charles Sims

THE ENGLISH CIVIL WAR
in 2 paragraphs

Charles I believed in the Divine Right of Kings (kings are appointed by God). In 1629 he dismissed the Parliament, which he despised. His queen, Henrietta Maria, was French and openly Catholic in mostly Protestant England. Under her influence, Charles I introduced religious reforms, promoting the **High Anglican Church** which was much closer to Catholicism than the 'low' – more common – version of Anglican Protestantism. In High Anglican churches carved-stone altars replaced simple wooden communion tables. *The Book of Common Prayer* (the Anglican Church worship guide) was republished in a High Anglican version. At this point Scottish Protestants rebelled, and taxes were raised for a war against the rebels. The Parliament was convened, then dissolved, then convened again. Next the Irish Catholics rebelled. England split between those who sided with the parliament – the **Parliamentarians** (nicknamed the **Roundheads**), and the supporters of the king, the **Royalists**. In 1642 a violent Civil War broke out.

In 1646, after the Royalists were defeated in the siege of Oxford, Charles escaped dressed as a servant and surrendered to the Scottish rebels. They sold him to the Parliamentarians for £100,000! The king was convicted of treason and beheaded in 1649. A republic, the Commonwealth of England, was proclaimed. In 1653 Oliver Cromwell, one of the Parliamentarian military commanders, was named Lord Protector of the Commonwealth, but after his death 5 years later the republic started falling apart, and in 1660 the monarchy was restored: Charles II, the son of Charles I, became king.

"Charles I" by Anthony van Dyck and "The Execution of King Charles I at Whitehall" by Ernest Crofts

By the 18th century the Scientific Revolution – the birth of modern science through the work of Copernicus, Newton, and other scholars – had put into question the view of the Earth as the center of the Universe. The discoveries of European explorers brought news of the great ancient civilizations in Asia, Africa and the Americas, and questioned the status of Europe as the God-appointed center of the world. New inventions were changing society and the economy of Europe. The **Industrial Revolution** began. From the agricultural areas people migrated to cities, becoming factory workers. The power of business owners was growing. With the printing press, education became more available. Knowledge no longer belonged to scholars and the privileged classes. Mass media was born, spreading ideas quickly through pamphlets and newspapers. This created what we now call **public opinion** and higher expectations regarding freedoms and civil rights for all.

The 17th century brought the **Age of Enlightenment** (also known as the **Age of Reason**) – an intellectual movement that put logic and scientific evidence above spiritual experiences and faith. Enlightenment thinkers rejected the idea that kings and governments are given authority by God. Instead, they promoted **Natural Law** ('Lex Naturalis' in Latin) – the idea that all human lives are equal before God, and should be equal in society. The success of the American Revolution – the creation of a republic and the adoption of the US constitution – proved that all these Enlightenment ideas could become reality. So, the *ideological* foundation (the system of ideas) for the French Revolution was ready.

Meanwhile, a massive social disaster was brewing in France. Its population grew from 18 to 26 million over the 18th century, with hundreds of thousands moving into cities from the countryside where peasants were under an enormous burden of taxes. There were taxes on candles, on firewood, on wine, on grain... The most awful was the salt tax. Every man, woman, and child over 7 had to buy 7 pounds of salt a year, at prices that never stopped rising. Meanwhile, in the cities the situation wasn't better. Out of 600,000 inhabitants of Paris, 1/3 were unemployed and lived in extreme poverty. The methods of growing crops on the farms were ancient and ineffective. There was a shortage of food – even at insanely high prices. Clearly, this couldn't last. But the system of absolute monarchy gave French kings the right to rule without consulting anyone, and King Louis XVI was just the type to take advantage of that. He was uninterested in governing and had his critics killed or imprisoned.

ABSOLUTE MONARCHY vs CONSTITUTIONAL MONARCHY

In an absolute monarchy, the monarch (king, queen, emperor, sultan...) has unlimited power. Under a constitutional (or 'parliamentary') monarchy, the monarch shares power with an elected government (such as a parliament) and rules only in keeping with the country's constitution.

THE SALT TAX

Taxation of salt first appeared in China, around 300 BC and was used to fund the building of the Great Wall of China. The French were the first to implement it in Europe in 1360. Many famous revolts were provoked by the salt tax. Among them are the 1631 Salt Revolt in Spain, the 1648 Moscow Salt Riot, and the 1930 Salt March in India led by Mahatma Gandhi.

THE FRENCH REVOLUTION *in 1 paragraph*

In 1789, brought to the edge of desperation by poverty and social injustice, the citizens of Paris stormed the Bastille prison – the symbol of the oppression they suffered under the French monarchy. France became a republic, executed its former king and queen, Louis XVI and Marie Antoinette, found itself at war with most of Europe, and went through a series of government changes and mass executions known as the **Reign of Terror**. During the Reign of Terror at least 17,000 'enemies of the revolution' were executed, over 10,000 died in prisons, and huge numbers of people perished during street clashes and violence. In 1799 French general Napoleon Bonaparte seized control of the army and in 1804, proclaimed himself emperor. His idea to unite Europe through conquest resulted in the endless **Napoleonic Wars**, but in 1812 Napoleon was defeated by Russia, then he lost Paris, was defeated again at Waterloo, Netherlands (1815), by allied European forces, and exiled. The French monarchy was restored: Louis XVIII, brother of Louis XVI, was placed on the throne of France.

"Storming of the Bastille" by Charles Thevenin

VOLTAIRE
1694 – 1778

Voltaire was one of the most prominent French writers and philosophers of the Age of Enlightenment. His criticism of the church and royal authority paved the way for the French Revolution. 'Voltaire' was the pen name of Francois-Marie Arouet. His father was a lawyer and wanted his son to follow in his footsteps. Voltaire, however, wanted to be a writer. So when his dad got him a job at a notary's office in Paris, Voltaire pretended to work, while actually spending his days writing poetry. His dad found out, was furious, and sent Voltaire to study law in Caen, Normandy (northern coast of France), but Voltaire kept writing more than studying. Mr. Arouet found another job for his son – as an assistant to the French Ambassador in The Hague, the Netherlands. But over there Voltaire fell in love with a protestant girl – a scandal! Fearing that Voltaire would abandon his Catholic faith, his boss sent him home to France.

Back in Paris Voltaire's witty and sarcastic criticisms of the government and the Catholic church grew popular. And the government noticed that. In 1717, at age 23, Voltaire was sentenced to imprisonment in the Bastille for his insulting jokes about the royal family. He spent a year in a cell with 10-foot-thick walls and no windows. Out of jail, Voltaire published plays, poetry, and pamphlets promoting religious tolerance, freedom of speech, and the idea of adopting a constitution. His fame spread quickly thanks to the culture of discussion and debate that emerged in Parisian coffee houses and reading clubs. This culture made Paris the intellectual center of France. The royal court at Versailles found itself isolated and lost its trend-setting influence.

COFFEE AND CAFES

Coffee is made from the roasted 'coffee beans' - the seeds of the tropical coffee bush growing in Africa and Asia. The drink was first brewed in Yemen in the 15th century and became popular all over the Arab world. The word "coffee" comes from the Arabic qahwa. In the 17th century coffee for the first time appeared in Europe, and coffeehouses (French "cafés") became clubs where the "reading public" discussed news and politics.

In 1726 an aristocratic bully made fun of Voltaire for adopting a pen name rather than writing under his real name. Voltaire responded by pointing out that the 'Voltaire' name was famous while the bully was a nobody despite his aristocratic name. The bully, however, was well-connected, and Voltaire ended up in the Bastille again, this time without trial!

He asked to replace his imprisonment with an exile and was allowed to leave for England where he spent two and a half years.

In 1729, the French government organized a lottery to pay off its debts. Voltaire's friend, the mathematician Charles de La Condamine, discovered an error in the lottery calculations: The prizes paid out by the government every month were larger than the value of all the tickets it sold! Voltaire and La Condamine organized mass purchases of the tickets and made a fortune. Now Voltaire was wealthy and dedicated all his time to writing.

Unlike France, England had a constitutional monarchy – with much more freedom of speech and religion. Inspired by the unrestricted political debate, Voltaire, in his writings, tore to shreds the outdated and worn-out European monarchies and mocked their royal families. Led by Voltaire, a new class of revolutionary *intellectuals* seized control of the *political narrative* in Europe. Fearing their criticism and ridicule, kings and queens lined up to flatter Voltaire and seek his approval. King George I of Great Britain awarded Voltaire with medals, Frederick the Great of Prussia (Germany) bragged of being his friend, and Russian Empress Catherine the Great corresponded with Voltaire for years, and after his death purchased his library. In France, however, King Louis XV banned Voltaire from Paris. Voltaire returned there only 25 years later, a few months before his death.

POLITICAL NARRATIVE

'Political narrative' is the way events are presented by politicians and media. For example, a few events can be interpreted as being connected by the same cause or the same consequences, so they are always mentioned together and form a 'story.' Using this story to persuade voters or shape public opinion turns it into a 'political narrative.'

"Voltaire at the Café Procope reading club" by Claudius Jacquand

French coffe pot, silver and ebony, 1757

Voltaire wasn't loyal to his new royal patrons. He was treated like a king at the court of Frederick the Great in Prussia, but this didn't prevent him from spying on Frederick for the French government. In 1743, hoping to be allowed to return to Paris, he proposed to the French to become their informant (spy), and wrote letters reporting on Frederick's private conversations and the state of his finances.

Voltaire never married and had no family and kids. He died at 83, in 1778, 11 years before the French Revolution. Because of his life-long criticism of the Catholic Church, Voltaire was not allowed to be buried with Christian rites. His friends buried him secretly in Champagne (a province in the East of France famous for its sparkling wines) at an abbey where the abbot was Voltaire's relative.

The mockery of Christian beliefs was, perhaps, Voltaire's darkest contribution to the human tragedy of the French Revolution. It prompted many intellectuals and politicians of his day to discard the ethics – ideas about right and wrong – based on Christianity, with nothing to replace them. The violence and mass executions of the revolutionary Reign of Terror happened in an ethical vacuum where the cost of human life hit rock bottom.

In 1767 Voltaire wrote to Frederick II, King of Prussia: "Our religion is certainly the most ridiculous, the most absurd and the most bloody religion which has ever infected this world. Your Majesty will do the human race an eternal service by destroying this infamous superstition – not among the street mobs, who are not worthy of being enlightened and who don't mind being oppressed, but among men who are thinkers." Claiming to be a defender of equality and tolerance, Voltaire despised common people and encouraged his 'educated' followers to hate their own countries – their values, faith, and culture. Referring to religion, Voltaire wrote, "Those who can make you believe absurdities, can make you commit atrocities." Yet 11 years after his death the atrocities of the French Revolution were committed by the 'men who are thinkers,' Voltaire's followers, who rejected Christianity, replaced it with the worship of liberty and equality, and proclaimed that "the end justifies the means."

Leaders of the French Revolution rightfully believed that it was Voltaire's ideas that made the revolution possible. In 1791, Voltaire's body was moved from Champagne to Paris and reburied at the Panthéon built as a church of St. Genevieve, the patron saint of Paris, and turned into a burial place of revolutionary leaders and 'heroes' of the revolution.

Voltaire was witty, and his writings are a source of many famous quotes. My favorite is, "Common sense is not all that common" *(The Pocket Philosophical Dictionary, 1764)*.

Some other quotes of Voltaire:
"Everything you say should be true, but not everything true should be said."
"It is dangerous to be right in matters where established men are wrong."
"The more often a stupidity is repeated, the more it sounds like wisdom."
"It is forbidden to kill. Therefore all murderers are punished unless they kill in large numbers and to the sound of trumpets."
"We are all guilty of the good we did not do."
"Judge a man by his questions rather than his answers."
"Encourage those who seek the truth but beware of those who find it."

The shoe Marie Antoinette lost on the steps of the scaffold where she was executed

The Hall of Mirrors at the Versailles Palace, 17-18th century

ROUSSEAU
1712 – 1778

Jean-Jacques Rousseau, one of the most prominent thinkers of the Age of Reason, was born in Geneva, Switzerland. His father was a watchmaker and a dance teacher. His mom died a few days after his birth. Geneva was a Calvinist Protestant city-state ruled – supposedly – by the democratic vote of its male citizens, but actually by a few wealthiest families that made up the city council. Rousseau's dad often worked all night assembling watches, and his son read to him, to keep him awake.

Rousseau's favorite book was *Lives of the Noble Greeks and Romans Compared* (also known as *Parallel Lives*) by the ancient Greek historian Plutarch. It gave him, in his own words, "the free and republican spirit."

As a 15-year-old, Jean-Jacques worked as an apprentice (a student-helper) to an engraver, but his boss beat him and one day the boy ran away. When he came back at night, the gates of Geneva were locked. Rousseau was offered shelter by a Catholic priest. The king of Piedmont, Italy, paid Catholics in Switzerland for each Protestant brought back to the Catholic faith. The priest and his friends convinced Rousseau to go to Italy and convert to catholicism. Calvinist Protestant doctrine focused on predestination – the idea that people have no free will and that some people are 'predestined' by God to be saved, while others are 'pre-condemned' for hell. This idea had never appealed to Rousseau. He preferred the teaching of the Catholic Church: People have free will, and if they repent, their sins can be forgiven through the sacrament of confession. After his conversion to Catholicism, Rousseau lost his Geneva citizenship and was rejected by his family. He lived first in Italy, then in France working as a servant and as a tutor.

In his late 20s Rousseau went to Paris, and, traveling on foot, he started noticing the extreme poverty of the French countryside. Once he stopped by a farmhouse, hoping to be offered some food, but the farmer, scared of tax collectors, pretended he had hardly anything. Only after a long conversation did he bring out some fine bread and sparkling wine he was hiding in the cellar. Both wine and bread were taxed, he explained. Rousseau was shocked and decided to become the defender of the poor.

In addition to taxes, French farmers had to do compulsory labor on the roads, which took them away from their fields and ruined them financially. Then there was also the property tax, and, since half of the land in France belonged to the king, the church, and the aristocracy, most farmers had to share their crops with the landlords. Hunting was reserved only for the nobility. And how about the so-called 'silence of the frogs' duty? ('silence des grenouilles,' in French) Peasants were obligated to prevent the croaking of the frogs at night to make sure they didn't wake up the landlord's wife. Instead of sleeping, the workers pounded on the water of the ponds and streams near the landlord's house with sticks to chase away the frogs. This duty could be replaced with a fine paid to the landlord.

In Paris, Rousseau was introduced to the court of Louis XV. A witty conversationalist, a good writer, and a composer of music, he became popular in Parisian salons – gatherings of aristocracy and intellectuals. Rousseau wrote 7 operas, and Louis XV's queen, Marie, performed in one of them. Rousseau's philosophical and political views started to take shape. He divided the evolution of human society into 3 stages. First there were cavemen – 'brute animals' who didn't value human life and were always at war. Next humans learned to work together and to live in equality and peace. Now they were 'noble savages.' Finally, civilization developed with its inequality, corruption, and more wars. "Equality disappeared," wrote Rousseau, "property was introduced, labor became necessary, and the vast forests changed to smiling fields that had to be watered with the sweat of men, where slavery and poverty were soon seen to germinate and grow along with the crops.

SALON

Salons were gatherings of academic intellectuals, artists, writers, aristocracy, politicians, and government leaders hosted by influential women from prominent families. They first appeared in Renaissance Italy, and flourished in Europe in the Enlightenment era and beyond. The term 'salon' comes from 'salone' – Italian for 'reception hall.' In salons guests exchanged gossip, news, and ideas. Their discussions often shaped the 'public opinion.'

"Molière reads his play 'Tartuffe' at a Parisian salon" by Nicolas-André Monsiau

The 'noble savage' living in harmony with nature is the ideal state for humanity, concluded Rousseau. "Civilization is a hopeless race to discover remedies for the evils it produces."

These ideas prompted Rousseau's philosophy of education. Young kids are guided mostly by emotion, he taught. Between 12 and 16 they develop the ability to reason. Kids are similar to 'noble savages' and should live close to nature and learn through play and hands-on projects. Instead of drilling math or Latin, education should focus on building character and the sense of right and wrong to prepare kids for life in the corrupt and hypocritical adult society. Kids should not be punished, taught Russeau. Instead, they should learn by observing the consequences of their behavior. So if a kid broke a window, don't punish him, and don't fix the window! If it's cold outside, just let the kid suffer from the cold, or put him in a room without windows, Rousseau suggested. Rousseau recommended that all kids should learn a work skill such as carpentry, that could save them from poverty in the future. Many parents in Paris adopted Rousseau's educational methods. In keeping with his recommendations, future King Louis XVI was taught the skill of a locksmith as a teenager.

Rousseau became an authority on education, and nobody cared to ask whether he himself had kids and how he raised them, except...Voltaire. Rousseau competed with Voltaire for the attention of the Parisian salons, and Voltaire was ruthless to his competitors. In 1764 he published an anonymous pamphlet stating that Rousseau had 5 kids all of whom he gave up for adoption as babies and never bothered to find out what happened to them. Rousseau was enraged and denied everything, but the rumors persisted, so he started writing his autobiography, *Confessions*, where he eventually admitted that Voltaire was right. Here is the story. After Rousseau settled in Paris, he met a hard-working lady, a seamstress, who supported her elderly mom and a bunch of siblings. Rousseau hired her as a servant. She became his girlfriend and over a few years they had 5 kids. He never married her, and took all their babies to an orphanage against her will. Why? In those days he was too poor to raise his kids, explained Rousseau. Then, fearing nobody would buy that, he came up with another, even more hypocritical explanation: His girlfriend's family was too uneducated, and he didn't want these common people to raise his kids..."I trembled at the thought of leaving them in the hands of a family so uneducated." Apparently in an orphanage they had better educational prospects than growing up with a famous intellectual for a father...

HYPOCRISY

Hypocrisy comes from the Greek hypokrisis "acting on the stage; pretending." A hypocrite is a pretender, a person whose actions contradict their words.

Art presenting symbols and ideas of the French revolutionary 'civil religion' – "Liberty Triumphant," 1792 (above) and "The Triumph of the French Republic," early 20th century

Rousseau set forth his political philosophy in his book *The Social Contract*. "Man is born free, but everywhere he is in chains," he wrote. Society enslaves people through property. The rich are free, the poor are slaves. The only way to overcome this inequality is to agree on a 'social contract': Everyone has to give up some freedom, and, instead of doing what they want, people should do what benefits their community as a whole. More than any other book of that era, *The Social Contract* inspired the leaders of the French Revolution. In France the book was banned. Even in Geneva – not a monarchy, but a republic ruled by the local 'oligarchs' (the super rich) – *The Social Contract* was banned and publicly burned. Voltaire, madly jealous of Rousseau, killed two birds with one stone with the following comment: "Burning this book was as disgusting as writing it."

But it was Rousseau's view of religion that got him in even deeper trouble. He believed that all religions are equally true if they lead people to God and teach them to do good. This religious philosophy – known as **Deism** – was popular in the Age of Enlightenment. It says that our knowledge of God comes only from our personal experience, not from sacred books or church teachings. "I perceive God everywhere in His works," Rousseau observed. " I sense Him in me; I see Him all around me." Rousseau also proposed the idea of a ***civil religion*** – a set of holidays and public rituals that promote patriotism. Civil religion became a big thing during the French Revolution, whose leaders hated Christianity. They shut down churches, melted down church bells, eliminated Sunday as the day of worship, destroyed crosses and wrote over the gates of cemeteries, "Death is an eternal sleep." They replaced Christianity with a 'civil religion' – the cult of the 'Goddess of Reason' who was worshiped at the 'temples of Reason' (former churches, including the famous Cathedral of Notre Dame in Paris).

The Archbishop of Paris condemned Rousseau for these ideas. A public burning of his books was held in Paris and the government issued a warrant for his arrest. Rousseau escaped to Geneva, but was kicked out of there as a traitor. He went to Prussia but local Protestants threw stones at him in the streets wherever he went. His house was attacked, all windows broken. He sailed to the tiny Swiss island of St.-Pierre, but he was soon run out of there as well. In 1766 he ended up in England, and that's when Voltaire struck again! He anonymously published a letter where he collected all the critical remarks Rousseau had ever made about England and the English monarchy. London newspapers ran with it. Rousseau was forced to return to France. For the rest of his life he stayed out of the spotlight and made his living by copying sheet music and giving music lessons.

ROBESPIERRE
1758 – 1794

Maximilien de Robespierre was one of the leaders of the French Revolution who steered it through years of violence and massive political change. Robespierre's father was a lawyer, his mom died when he was 6. A local bishop who was a friend of his family arranged a scholarship for Robespierre at one of the best schools in Paris. And so it was that Robespierre left home at age 11. Studying Roman literature, law and rhetoric (speech-making) in Latin, he embraced the ideas of democracy and admired Cato, Cicero, Brutus, and other leaders of the Roman Republic. He was concerned about the rights of the working people and the poor, hated the wealthy and the privileged, and one of his favorite books was *The Social Contract* by Rousseau. In 1776, during Robespierre's school years, the American colonies adopted the Declaration of Independence. France supported the United States against Britain, and many Frenchmen left for America to defend the American Revolution in the ranks of the Continental Army. They returned home inspired by the victory of the colonists over the British monarchy. A spirit of revolution was spreading across Europe.

Robespierre studied law at Sorbonne University, and at 24 was appointed a criminal court judge in his native region of Arras. Despite the prestige of this position, Robespierre soon quit, because – thanks to the influence of Rousseau – he was opposed to the death penalty. Only 10 years later, however, he would declare that, for the revolution to win, King Louis XVI had to be executed. He would also sign hundreds of death sentences.

In 1788, the king announced elections to the French General Assembly, a body that had not met for 175 years. It was the gathering of the representatives of the 3 'estates' or groups of citizens – the clergy (representatives of the church), the noblemen, and the common people. Robespierre was elected one of the 600 representatives of the Third Estate, the common people, who made up 96% of the nation. The representatives of the Third Estate demanded that the nobles and clergy should pay taxes. When their proposals were rejected, they quit the General Assembly and formed the National Assembly. The king didn't recognize it and ordered the Assembly dismissed, but the representatives of the people refused to leave.

Meanwhile, there were rumors that the king had sent his army to take Paris and to massacre the National Assembly. Riots broke out in the streets. The carriages of the nobility and the wealthy were attacked. The rioters were the **sans-culottes**, urban workers driven to extreme poverty after a hail storm damaged grain crops in 1788, causing bread prices to skyrocket.

Huge crowds of sans-culottes in the streets of Paris shouted "To arms! To arms!" They broke into armories, armed themselves with swords and muskets, and attached red-and-blue **cockades** – knots of ribbons – to their hats so they could tell who was on the side of the revolution and who wasn't. The king's generals were afraid to face the angry crowds, and by the morning of July 14, 1789, the whole of Paris was armed. The fury of the sans-culottes was directed against the Bastille – the ancient prison fortress with a double moat and massive walls they viewed as a symbol of tyranny.

Revolutionary crowds besieged and stormed the Bastille. Its commander surrendered and was killed. Inside there were only 7 prisoners, who were carried around Paris like heroes. The Duke de La Rochefoucauld, an aristocratic deputy of the Assembly, informed King Louis XVI, "Your Majesty, the Bastille has fallen."
"This is a revolt!" exclaimed the king.
The duke responded with his famous phrase, "No, it's not a revolt, it is a revolution."

COCKADE ('COCARDE' in French)

The French word 'cocarde' comes from coq – rooster – perhaps because it looks like a rooster's crest. A cockade is a badge made of ribbons and worn on a hat. The ribbon colors – like colors of national flags – indicate the political affiliation of the wearer. French revolutionaries adopted the colors of the coat of arms (the emblem) of Paris: red and blue on the background of 'constitutional' white.

THE SANS-CULOTTES

Culottes were knee-length silk breeches – pants worn by 18th-century nobles and city professionals. Working people were often referred to as sans-culottes – the 'pantless' – because they didn't wear the breeches. Instead, they wore long pants that were considered 'low class.' Throughout the French Revolution the sans-culottes were its driving force. Whoever had their support, ruled France.

"A sans-culotte" by Louis-Leopold Boilly and a 'cocarde tricolore,' early 19th century

The National Assembly adopted *The Declaration of the Rights of Man and of the Citizen* proclaiming equal rights for all, freedom of speech and of religion. The original text of the Declaration was written by Marquis de Lafayette, a French officer who had fought in the American Revolutionary War. Lafayette was friends with George Washington and Thomas Jefferson. Jefferson helped him with the draft of the Declaration. Meanwhile, France was shaken by dozens of riots – peasants, soldiers, and sans-culottes rebelled in every corner of the country.

Robespierre's authority among the revolutionaries grew. He was supported by the so-called **Jacobin Club** – the Society of the Friends of the Constitution, a 1200-member political group in Paris that met at an abandoned Dominican (or 'Jacobin') convent. Robespierre's every speech at the Jacobin Club focused on one idea: France is overrun by traitors and spies, and the only way to save the revolution is to round up anyone suspicious and send them to the **guillotine**. The sans-culottes and the Jacobins admired Robespierre. He was nicknamed 'the Incorruptible.' Hundreds of aristocrats – men and women alike – and wealthy business owners were executed with or without trial. All church property and the property of the executed 'enemies of the republic' was confiscated and sold to raise money for the revolutionary army.

"French poet André Chénier and other victims of the Reign of Terror at the Saint-Lazare prison" by Charles Louis Müller

In 1791 King Louis XVI and his family escaped from the Tuileries Palace and attempted to leave France, but were stopped at Varennes and returned to Paris. The king was forced to wear a red **liberty cap** and drink to the health of Revolutionary France. A year later the revolutionary National Guard and crowds of sans-culottes attacked the Tuileries Palace and massacred the royal Swiss Guards. The king and his family were imprisoned in the Temple, a gloomy fortress built in the 13th century by the Knights Templar.

"Louis XVI at the Temple" by Ambroise Louis Garneray; below: Louis XVI wears a liberty cap

THE GUILLOTINE

A machine used to behead criminals was invented in Italy. It was adopted in France by Louis XVI on the recommendation of a prominent Enlightenment-era intellectual Dr. Guillotin, and was nicknamed La Guillotine. Joseph Guillotin was a medical doctor and a deputy of the revolutionary National Assembly. Ironically, he was executed by guillotine during the Reign of Terror.

Eventually France was declared a republic and Robespierre started to promote the idea that the king should face trial and be executed. In January of 1793, after a staged 'trial,' the king was beheaded by the guillotine in a public square.

THE LIBERTY CAP

In Ancient Rome a **pileus** (a conical felt cap) was given to freed slaves during the ceremony of manumission (setting free, from **manu mittere** – 'to release by hand'). The slave's head was shaved and pileus was worn as a symbol of **libertas** ('freedom' in Latin) – the status of being a Roman citizen, which included (for men) the right to vote. A similar hat, with the tip pulled forward, was worn by Persians and other inhabitants of Western Asia. Ancient Greeks called it the Phrygian cap after Phrygia, the ancient kingdom on the territory of modern Turkey. During the American Revolution the Phrygian cap got mixed up with the pileus and was worn as a symbol of freedom. French revolutionaries adopted it too.

King Louis XVI addresses the crowd before his execution; Below: "Marie Antoinette on her way to the execution" by Francois Flameng

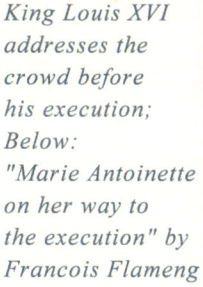

"Frenchmen, I die innocent! I pardon my enemies!" were the last words of Louis XVI. Soon the queen, Marie Antoinette, was sentenced to death and executed. Sans-culottes hunted the royalists (supporters of royal power) and broke into wealthy homes. The prisons were packed. The lists of those condemned to death ("Those who have gained prizes in the lottery of Sainte-Guillotine") were read out loudly under the prison windows causing panic among prisoners to the amusement of the jailors. The 'enemies' were brought in carts, hands tied, to the guillotine, often unaware of charges against them. The executions averaged about 30 a day. Throughout the revolution, executions became popular entertainment. Large crowds attended them every day and the front seats were always claimed by women, known as "the knitters." The knitters sat in front of the guillotine all day knitting socks for their families and gossiping.

Citizens were encouraged to rat on one another. Some made it their profession to hang out in cafes making lists of 'suspects.' Students were beheaded for using educated ('aristocratic') language, workers – for drinking wine on a day when the revolutionary army suffered a defeat, peasant girls were beheaded for humming a 'royalist song', kids – for having been born into a wealthy family, grandmas – for crying over the victims...

The Reign of Terror began and spread all over France. Over 300,000 people were arrested and thrown in jail during the Reign of Terror – 1 in 50 was a 'traitor.' In the Vendee, in Western France, royalist rebels – men, women, and children – were executed by the hundreds. Since the guillotine wasn't fast enough, whole barges of captives were drowned in the river Loire. And when they ran out of ships, they started tying prisoners in pairs and tossing them into the river. This was called 'a Republican marriage.' At least 15 thousand were drowned. The Loire kept carrying corpses down to the sea for several months.

The National Assembly, now called the Convention, ruled France like a dictatorship, and Robespierre ruled the Convention. All titles were abolished, every citizen of France – man or woman – was addressed as 'Citizen.' The usual calendar was replaced by the 'Republican Calendar' purged of all references to religious or historical events. September 22, 1792, the day when the French Republic was proclaimed, became the first day of the revolutionary 'era.' Months were renamed. New spring months were Germinal (when seeds germinate), Floreal (when flowers bloom) and Prairial (from French *prairie* – a meadow). New summer months were Messidor (from Latin *messis* – harvest), Thermidor (from Greek *thermon* – heat), and Fructidor (from Latin *fructus* – fruit)...and so on. Each month was made of 3 weeks, 10 days each. The revolutionaries introduced decimal time. Each day was 10 hours, each hour 100 minutes, each minute 100 seconds. New watches and clocks were manufactured, but people didn't seem enthusiastic about these innovations.

Churches were replaced with 'Temples of Reason.' A new holiday, the 'Feast of Reason' was appointed in place of Christmas and Easter.

"The Feast of Reason at the Notre Dame Cathedral in Paris on Nov.10, 1793" by Charles Louis Muller (the foot of the 'goddess' is on the crucifix)

Notre Dame (Our Lady) Cathedral in Paris – turned into a Temple of Reason – held 'ceremonies' that were ghastly parodies of Christian liturgy. An opera dancer dressed in sky blue and crowned with a wreath of oak leaves was brought to the cathedral on a golden chariot and seated on the high altar. The 'worshippers' bowed down before the new goddess, while young girls showered her with flowers, singing revolutionary songs...In the Church of Saint Eustache the services were replaced with drunken feasts. Tables with sausages, pastries and wine were set, and everyone was invited. The 'worshippers' quickly got drunk and hardly paid attention to another 'Goddess of Reason' in blue sitting on the church altar guarded by armed sans-culottes. Outside the church the intoxicated crowds danced around the bonfire where church pews and other church furniture were burned.

Every day Robespierre called to "purify the Republic of France by blood" at the Jacobin Club. The club's galleries were overflowing with spectators who screamed "Liberty! Equality! Fraternity!" and wildly applauded their hero. Robespierre lived all alone on the fourth floor of a building on Rue Saint-Honoré (*rue* = 'street' in French). His landlords didn't let anyone in, including Robespierre's sister Charlotte who had fallen into poverty and sought a shelter. One day, when Robespierre was leaving Convention hall, his fans placed a crown of oak leaves on his head, unharnessed the horses from his carriage, and rolled it themselves all the way to his home, shouting "Behold the friend of the people! Behold the defender of liberty!"

Robespierre noticed that many – even among the revolutionaries – were shocked at the Temple of Reason 'services', but few dared to protest. So the time came for the organizers of those ceremonies to be sent to the guillotine! Robespierre decided to try his own hand at creating a new 'civil religion.' The Goddess of Reason was replaced with the cult of the 'Supreme Being' and the 'martyrs of Liberty.' Robespierre was its High Priest.

The Festival of the Supreme Being in Paris

In June 1794, the Tuileries garden was crowded with people for the new religious 'ceremony.' Everyone wore wreath crowns: ivy and olive branches for the old people, oak for the middle-aged, myrtle for the youth, and violets for kids. Robespierre arrived in a sky-blue coat carrying a bouquet of flowers and ears of wheat. Cardboard figures representing Atheism, Discord, and Selfishness, designed by the famous painter and revolutionary David, were set on fire by Robepierre and from behind them rose the figure of Wisdom, badly blackened by the smoke.

"Today let us enjoy ourselves, tomorrow we will begin afresh to fight the enemies of the Republic," said Robespierre in his speech. Many thought the 'ceremony' was ridiculous and awkward, and laughed at Robespierre. He noticed every smirk and grin and didn't forgive. The Convention also declared another national holiday – the anniversary of the execution of Louis XVI, and ordered the destruction of the tombs of the kings of France at the Basilica of Saint-Denis.

Robespierre survived an assassination attempt. A 20-year-old girl Cecile Renault, who believed Robespierre was a godless tyrant, came to Rue Saint-Honoré and asked to see him. His landlord was suspicious and didn't let her in. Cecile was seized and searched. She had knives and a new beautiful dress in her basket. She confessed to the assassination attempt and said the dress was for her to wear to the guillotine. To humiliate her, the revolutionary judge made her wear filthy beggar's rags to her trial and execution. That's how petty and vengeful the revolution had become. Cecile wasn't upset and 'died cheerfully' according to witnesses.

Once all the prominent aristocrats, royalists and other 'enemies of the people' were sent to the guillotine, the French Revolution did what all revolutions do: It turned against its own. 'Purges' began among the revolutionaries themselves. More moderate and less bloodthirsty political groups, like the *Girondists*, were arrested and the heads of yesterday's revolutionaries rolled right and left. Danton, Robespierre's friend, a president of the Jacobin Club, and the founder of the Revolutionary Tribunal, dared to question whether all those imprisoned and condemned to death were, indeed, the enemies of the republic. Right away the tribunal he had founded sentenced him to death, Robespierre signed the sentence, and to the guillotine Danton went!

As the cart carrying him to the execution passed by Robespierre's house, Danton said "You will follow us shortly." His last words to the executioner were, "Show the people my head. It's worth seeing!" This is when Dr. Guillotin himself was 'guillotined.'

After a while, however, people began to complain that they were worse off than they had been under Louis XVI. Fingers were pointing at Robespierre. On Thermidor 8, Year II of the French Republic (July, 1794) Robespierre made a speech at the Convention condemning internal enemies and conspirators within the Convention. He didn't name names, so every deputy of the Convention expected to be arrested any day.

"The Convention rises against Robespierre" by Max Adamo Sturz

"Robespierre at the Hôtel de Ville on the night of 9 to 10 Thermidor Year II" by Jean-Joseph Weerts

While Robespierre was enjoying a dinner party that night, one of the deputies found Robespierre's coat hanging in the hallway and searched its pockets. There he found a list of forty names, including his own. He warned others and fled. The next day the deputies whom Robespierre intended to execute turned the Convention against him. Robespierre argued until he lost his voice. "It is the blood of Danton which chokes you!" shouted the deputies. This reminder of Robespierre's betrayal of Danton decided his fate. When the officers of the Convention were about to seize him, Robespierre grabbed a musket and attempted to shoot himself, but instead only broke his lower jaw.

"Wounded Robespierre" by Lucien-Étienne Mélingue

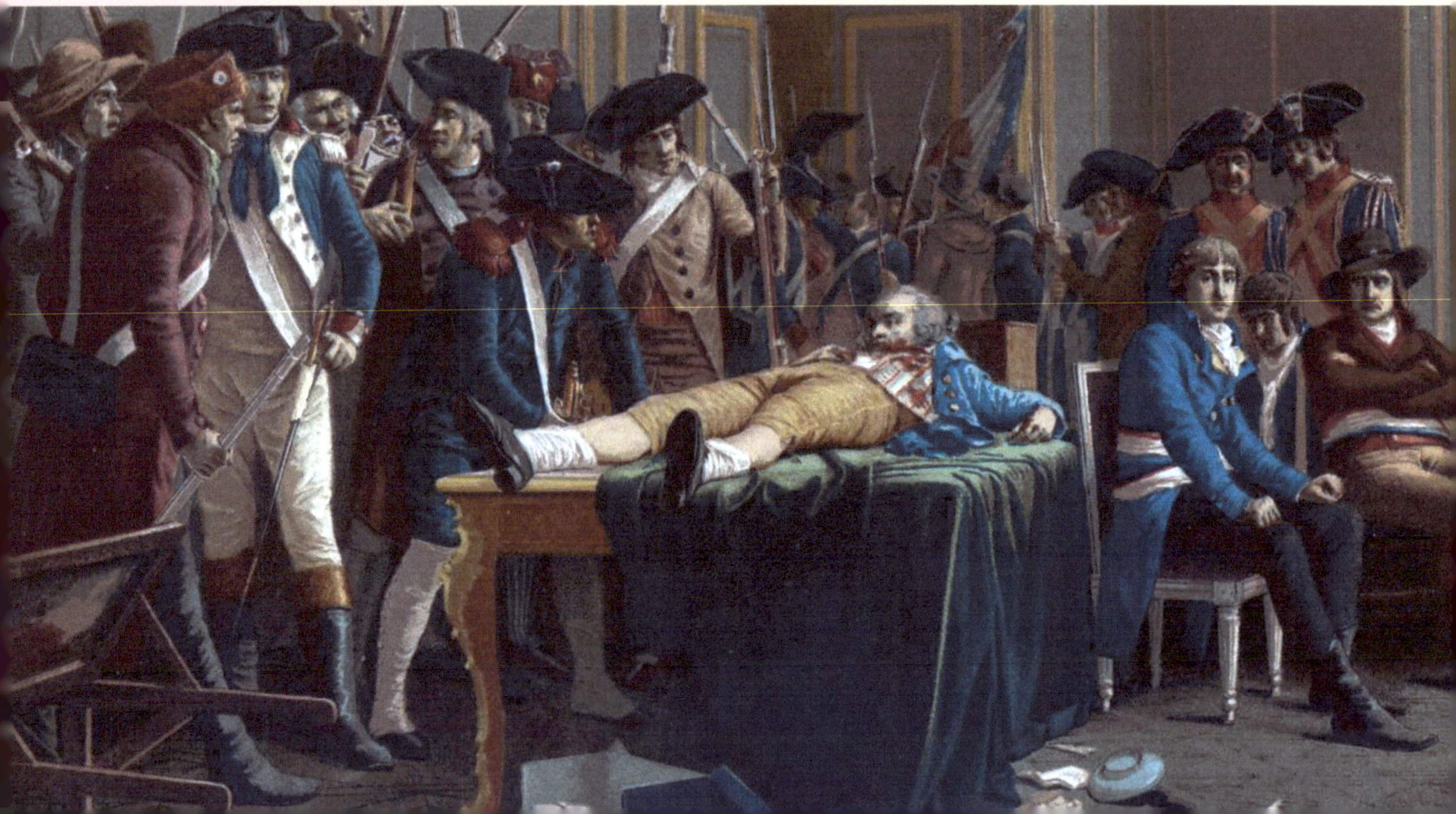

Arrest and execution of Robespierre; Right: "Robespierre on his way to the guillotine" by Alfred Muillard

Paris authorities were on the side of Robespierre. The city prisons refused to accept him, so the Convention sent him to the guillotine the very next day. Wives and mothers of revolutionaries sentenced to death by Robespierre danced around the cart that took him to execution. Friends of his victims cursed him along the way, and when he was beheaded, the spectators clapped loudly.

On a stone over Robespierre's grave someone scratched the following 'epitaph' (inscription on a tombstone): *Lament not, that I lie in my last bed,*
For, were I living, friend, you would be dead.

to lament = to complain

After Robespierre's death, prisons were opened, and 20,000 captives were set free. Interestingly, among the prisoners who would have died within the next few days, had Robespierre lived, was Josephine, the future wife of Napoleon Bonaparte and Empress of France.

LA MARSEILLAISE

Many of the revolutionary National Guard volunteers were from the South of France, from Marseille. They marched around Paris singing a new 'war song' composed by the revolutionary army officer Rouget de Lisle. The song was nicknamed the Marseillaise and eventually became the national anthem of France.

"Rouget de Lisle sings la Marseillaise for the first time" by Isidore Alexandre Pils

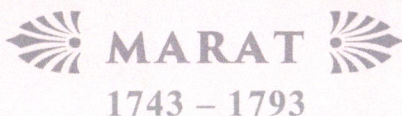

❋ MARAT ❋
1743 – 1793

❋ CHARLOTTE CORDAY ❋
1768 – 1793

More than anyone else, political writer and journalist Jean-Paul Marat shaped the 'narrative' of the French Revolution. His views were among the most *radical* (extreme) among the revolutionaries. He was the voice of the sans-culottes, and didn't hesitate to call desperately-poor and angry urban workers to revolutionary violence.

"Charlotte Corday" by Jean-Jacques Hauer, painted before her execution

"Artist Jean-Jacques Hauer & Charlotte Corday" by Arturo Michelena

Every revolution has its own **political narrative** – a 'storyline' explaining why this or that group of people would benefit from rising against the existing political system. The revolutionary 'narrative' is shaped and spread by **agitators** – activists who call people out onto the streets to protest, take up arms, and so on. Thinkers of the Enlightenment laid the **ideological** foundation, the set of ideas that drove the political movements of the Age of Revolutions. But it was the birth of mass media – pamphlets, newspapers, and journals – that made the revolutionary **agitation** possible. Political **pundits** (opinion makers, writers) and journalists started by promoting the ideas of Voltaire and Rousseau, and moved on to creating the 'storyline,' the political narrative of the Revolution – that drove people to action.

The narrative included

- blame, finding a *scapegoat* – blaming the social and economic disaster in France on one group – the king and the royalists;
- *fear-mongering* – sowing panic by telling the public that royalists and foreign invaders are coming to massacre anyone who supports the revolution;
- dividing people, organizing *witch hunts* – convincing the public that the revolutionary movement is infiltrated by traitors and spies... and so on.

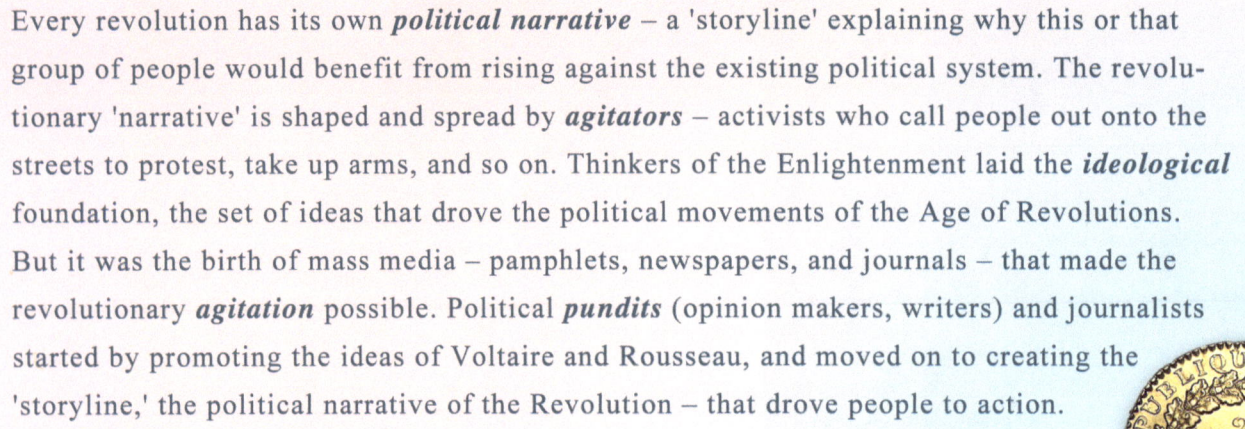

Revolutionaries: "Robespierre, Danton, and Marat" by Alfred Laudet

Marat started his career as a doctor and a scientist. In one of his scientific works, *Research into the Physics of Fire*, Marat tried to prove that fire was an 'igneous fluid' that 'leaked' from hot objects. Bizarrely, he claimed he saw it 'leak' from the head of Benjamin Franklin when he visited Paris in 1777! Marat asked the French Academy of Sciences to endorse (approve and recommend) his work. His ideas, however, didn't impress Antoine Lavoisier, the 'father of modern chemistry' and a member of the Academy. Lavoisier's greatest discovery was the role of oxygen in the chemical reaction of combustion (burning). He described and named oxygen and hydrogen. You can imagine what he thought of Marat's 'igneous' fluid seeping from Ben Franklin's head... In addition, Lavoisier was a wealthy nobleman, just the type Marat couldn't stand. Another star of French science, the great mathematician Laplace, supported Lavoisier against Marat. As a result, Marat's scientific career was over.

As the French Revolution started, Marat was 46. He gave up science for journalism and started publishing a newspaper, *L'Ami du Peuple* (*Friend of the People*, in French).

"Marat" by Lucien Etienne Melingue

A portrait of Lavoisier and his wife by Jacques-Louis David

SCAPEGOAT

The term 'scapegoat' comes from a ritual of Ancient Israel in which the High Priest of the Temple symbolically placed the sins of the people on a goat. The goat was then sent into the wilderness as a sacrifice,'carrying away' the blame for their wrongdoings.

L'Ami du Peuple wasn't a real newspaper – rather a multi-page *agitation* and *propaganda* pamphlet. Marat, a revolutionary *propagandist*, wrote all the 8 pages of his 'newspaper' himself every day, linking his reports into a persuasive 'storyline.' After the storming of the Bastille the king considered reforms, but Marat declared them a conspiracy. One of his headlines read, "A plot uncovered to lull the people to sleep." The article demanded the overthrow of the monarchy. Next, his newspaper published a report about a banquet held by the Versailles Palace military garrison to welcome new members. Marat claimed that during the banquet, drunken officers stamped with their boots on the symbol of the revolution, the *cocarde tricolore* – red-white-and-blue ribbon cockade. They also, supposedly, served rare and expensive delicacies at the banquet, while ordinary workers

PROPAGANDA AND AGENDA

Propaganda is any communication whose goal is to influence or persuade the audience to follow the *agenda* of the *propagandist*. An agenda is a set of talking points and goals. Both terms come from Latin:
agenda - things to be done
propaganda - things to be spread, propagated, disseminated

in Paris spent more than half of their salaries on overpriced stale bread. From propaganda Marat went straight to agitation and called for a march on Versailles, where the royal family lived in luxury and "sucked the blood" of the French people. Thousands of women who had assembled on the squares of Paris to protest the high bread prices heard of Marat's idea and joined the march. It became known as the Women's March on Versailles.

Armed with kitchen knives, women gathered in huge crowds, beating military marching drums. They forced a couple churches to ring their bells. Demanding weapons, they broke into the Hôtel de Ville (the City Hall of Paris) and plundered it. Under a pouring rain, the crowds of up to 10 thousand women headed to the royal residence – the Palace of Versailles. Louis XVI received the representatives of the women's march, impressed them with his charm, and promised free food.

Meanwhile, Marquis de Lafayette, the hero of the American War of Independence and one of the leaders of the French Revolution, arrived in Versailles with the revolutionary National Guard he commanded. His task was to prevent violence. Despite his anti-monarchy views, Lafayette was so overwhelmed at the opportunity to see the king, that he introduced himself with the words "I've come to die at the feet of Your Majesty." Louis approved. Lafayette was his kind of revolutionary! Outside, however, Lafayette's soldiers made

"Marquis de Lafayette" by Gilbert du Motier and "Louis XVI" by Joseph Duplessis

friends with the women rioters and, after some partying and some wine, at 6:00am soldiers and women together broke into the palace, killing royal guards, and demanding that the king go with them to Paris.

To calm down the drunk, raging crowd, the king and Lafayette showed up on the balcony. The king quickly agreed to go to Paris. The women demanded to see the queen. Marie Antoinette appeared on the balcony with her kids. The women yelled, "No kids!" This sounded like they considered violence against the queen. Lafayette and the king panicked, royal children rushed inside. But Marie Antoinette stood calm, hands crossed on her chest, looking right in the faces of the rioters. Stunned with her courage, the crowd backed off and fell silent. Lafayette melted in admiration, kneeled, and kissed the queen's hand. That was the end of the march. Everyone, including the royal family, went to Paris.

The Women's March on Versailles was the first riot incited by Marat. More followed. His calls to violence scared even the revolutionaries. At one point, the Paris authorities tried to arrest him, but the crowd of sans-culottes prevented the arrest and Marat escaped to London. He soon returned but was forced to hide in Paris sewers where he contracted a skin disease that tortured him for the rest of his life. Meanwhile his 'newspaper' kept shaping the narrative of the revolution. It provoked panic, publishing rumors that dozens of thousands of royalist soldiers were coming to slaughter the people of Paris, that folk in the countryside were dying of famine... Day after day, Marat demanded death for the aristocrats and 'counter-revolutionaries.' "Five or six hundred heads cut off would have guaranteed freedom and happiness," he wrote in July 1790. In the summer of 1792 the revolutionary government of Paris formed a Committee on Surveillance whose goal was to identify and eliminate the enemies of the revolution. This committee was to become the main driving force of the Reign of Terror of 1793-94. Marat was its most influential member. The Committee on Surveillance immediately zeroed in on the first group of 'suspects' and 4000 people were sent into prisons. They included aristocratic and wealthy families and even some revolutionaries now labeled *counter-revolutionaries*.

In September 1792 a mass killing of political prisoners, known as the September Massacres, occurred in Paris. The murderers were armed gangs made of foreign *mercenaries* (soldiers-for-hire), Parisian sans-culottes, and criminals convicted of violent crimes and released by the revolutionary government. On the orders of the Committee on Surveillance, they went from prison to prison, holding a few-minute *tribunals* and then killing hundreds of political prisoners by beating and hacking them to death in the prison courtyards. Among the victims were kids, as young as 10 years old. 220 were priests who stayed loyal to the Catholic Church.

surveillance = observing, monitoring, spying ; tribunal = an informal trial, a fast trial

Marat (in red jacket) at the Committee on Surveillance. Behind him is artist Jacques-Louis David, also a member of the committee. The 6th member of the committee was Danton (already dead!) The man on the left holds in his hand the "Certificate of Civism." The Committee issued these certificates as proof that a person was politically on the side of the revolution and couldn't be arrested as a traitor.

Marat not only defended this violence, but demanded more. In a document signed by Marat, the Committee on Surveillance encouraged revolutionaries in provincial France to follow the example of Paris, round up and kill 'traitors.' The violence spread all across France. Marat was elected the head of the Jacobin Club. Not everyone among the revolutionaries, however, agreed with the Jacobins. The Convention deputies known as the ***Girondists*** (most of them came from Gironde in southwest France) were terrified of being labeled 'traitors' by Marat and condemned the September Massacres. In the spring of 1793, under the influence of the Girondists, the Convention voted to arrest Marat, but the Revolutionary Tribunal cleared him of all charges.

A few months later Marat directed sans-culottes to storm the hall of the Convention and arrest the Girondists. The next day, 21 of them were taken in an old creaky cart to the execution. It was the same cart that took Louis XVI, Marie Antoinette, and thousands of 'royalists' to the guillotine. While awaiting their turn to be killed, the Girondists heroically sang the *Marseillaise* to prove their devotion to the revolution. As one head after another rolled, their chorus was getting quieter and quieter. One of the Girondists managed to commit suicide on the way to the execution. But that didn't stop the 'revolutionary justice.' The corpse of the hapless Girondist was beheaded with the rest!

Sans-culottes arrive to seize the Girondists

The Girondists arrive for their execution singing La Marseillaise... one of the Girondists lies in the cart – dead... the 'knitters' gossip on a raised platform under the umbrellas

Like many revolutions, the French Revolution started by uniting rebels against the old regime. But eventually, as they sorted themselves into different camps and started fighting for power, the revolution began 'devouring its own children.'

Marat didn't forget his personal enemies either. He wrote pamphlets calling Lavoisier a charlatan, a royalist and a traitor. Eventually revolutionaries shut down the Academy of Sciences. As the Jacobins seized power in revolutionary France, Marat was at the peak of his celebrity. His days, however, were numbered.

> **"THE REVOLUTION, LIKE SATURN, DEVOURS ITS OWN CHILDREN"**
>
> This saying became common during the French Revolution. In Greek and Roman mythology Saturn ('Kronos' in Greek) was a titan, the ruler of the Earth. He learned of a prophecy that he would be overthrown by one of his sons. So he ate his sons as soon as they were born. One of them, Zeus, was hidden by his mother, Rhea. When he grew up, he defeated his father and became the king of gods, fulfilling the prophecy.

On July 9, 1793, a 25-year-old woman from Normandy, Charlotte Corday, arrived in Paris, carrying with her nothing but a copy of Plutarch's *Lives of the Noble Greeks and Romans*. In Paris she went to a market and bought a kitchen knife with a 6-inch (15 cm) blade. Charlotte Corday was a supporter of the Girondists. She believed that because of Marat the revolution had taken a wrong turn. Armed with the knife, Charlotte went to Marat's house pretending she wanted to tell him about the Girondist 'traitors' who had escaped from Paris to her town of Caen, Normandy. Marat's skin disease was so painful that he spent most of his time in a bath with medicinal herbs and received his fans and friends sitting in a bathtub with a covered top. Charlotte Corday was invited to see Marat and assassinated him a few minutes into their conversation. Sentenced to the guillotine, she said,
"I killed one man to save a hundred thousand and to bring relief to my country."
Witnesses said she smiled all the way from prison to the guillotine.

"The assassination of Marat" by Jean-Joseph Weerts

A German revolutionary, Adam Lux, was present at the execution of Charlotte Corday and was so struck by her courage, that he threatened to kill himself in front of the National Convention to protest the Reign of Terror. He was executed a few days later.

"Charlotte Corday" by Paul Baudry
Below: Adam Lux, Charlotte Corday

Marat became the 'martyr' and the 'saint' of the Revolution. He was buried in the Panthéon. His embalmed heart in an urn was placed on an altar built in his memory at one of the revolutionary clubs. His sculptural portraits replaced crucifixes in the churches of Paris that became 'Temples of Supreme Being.' Robespierre also 'avenged' Marat by arresting Lavoisier. From prison Lavoisier wrote a letter to Benjamin Franklin, asking for help. He begged the revolutionary court to give him a couple days so he could write down a discovery he had made. The judge responded, "The Revolution has no need for scientists." Off to the guillotine went the 'father of modern chemistry.' He was beheaded and buried in a mass grave.

However, after the execution of Robespierre, the mood in the French society changed. The body of Marat was removed from Panthéon and his statues destroyed. Newspapers reported that kids dumped one of them into the sewer shouting, "Here is your Panthéon, Marat!" Lavoisier's widow was given an official document admitting that her husband was executed on false charges.

KING LOUIS XVI
1754 – 1793

QUEEN MARIE ANTOINETTE
1755 – 1793

Maria Theresa, Empress of Germany, had 16 kids. Her youngest child was Maria Antonia. No matter how hard her teachers tried, at 10 Maria Antonia couldn't write in German, her native language, but she played the harp, harpsichord, and flute like a professional musician. Maria Antonia was 14 when her royal parents changed her name to the French 'Marie Antoinette' and arranged her marriage to the Dauphin of France, the future King Louis XVI. Louis was 15. The marriage was a political deal to guarantee the peace treaty between Austria and France. When Marie Antoinette arrived in Paris, her French ladies-in-waiting (royal assistants) dressed her up in accordance with the latest fashion of the royal court and took her to meet Louis. Two days later they were married. At the wedding ceremony Marie signed the register in big childish handwriting, and French courtiers sneered, noticing she couldn't spell her own name. Once the wedding was over, the 'husband' and the 'wife' lived their own lives as if marriage had never happened.

Louis was kind, but shy and awkward. He loved maps and astronomy, went hunting every day, and was not interested in Marie Antoinette. Four years later, in 1774, the old king Louis XV (grandfather of Louis XVI) died of smallpox. When young Louis heard the news, he was horrified. "But we are too young to reign!" he exclaimed. Then Louis and Marie Antoinette – a 20 and a 19-year-old – cried and prayed together. The fear of the future brought them closer to each other. The coronation ceremony was held in the ancient town of Rheims where all French kings (except Henri IV) were crowned. Seven times the Archbishop poured precious ointment on Louis' head, calling out "Vivat rex in aeternum" (Latin for 'May the King live forever!'). Then he handed the scepter to the new king – Louis XVI.

Both Louis and Marie Antoinette were into serious luxury. Louis gave his wife the Petit Trianon, a small **château** (a mansion) on the palace grounds of Versailles, and gossipers reported she had covered its walls in pure gold.

DAUPHIN

Dauphin is a title that was given to the eldest son of the King of France because in the Middle Ages kings' eldest sons ruled the Dauphiné – a province in southeastern France. 'Dauphin' (doh-fen) means 'dolphin' in French. The rulers of the Dauphiné had a dolphin on their coat of arms and adopted 'dauphin' as their title.

Her 'poufs' – elaborate hair arrangements, decorated with flowers, feathers and jewels – were 3 ft (90cm)-high. In 1775 France was shaken by riots caused by the rising bread prices. Marie Antoinette's mom, Maria Theresa, wrote to her daughter suggesting that she try a more modest lifestyle, so as not to anger the poor. Predictably, Marie Antoinette ignored her. The winter of 1776 was dreadfully cold. Deep snow covered Paris. Many poor and homeless froze to death, while Marie and her court ladies rode around town singing in gilded sleds with silver bells. Marie Antoinette was a foreigner – they called her "the Austrian" – and an easy target. Future revolutionaries started building their 'narrative' about her – the storyline that can be summed up in the famous phrase "Let them eat cake."

"LET THEM EAT CAKE" WAS FAKE NEWS!

Did Marie Antoinette actually say the epic words attributed to her "Let them eat cake"? Supposedly, it was her response to a report that there was a shortage of bread and people were starving. The truth is, it's extremely unlikely Marie Antoinette ever said these words. They first appeared in Rousseau's book "Confessions" which he finished in 1767 – 3 years before Marie Antoinette arrived in France and married Louis. "I recalled the solution offered by a great princess," wrote Rousseau, "who was told that peasants had no bread, and who responded: Let them eat brioche." Brioche is soft bread made with a lot of butter and egg mixed into the dough. Even if Rousseau added these words to his book later, referring to Marie Antoinette, he is the only source of this story, so scholars think Rousseau just came up with it, and revolutionary journalists-agitators ran with it.

In cafes and salons all across France the followers of Voltaire and Rousseau called for the abolition of the absolute monarchy, for the constitution. In America they adopted the Declaration of Independence. When Benjamin Franklin came to Paris in 1777 to ask Louis XVI for help against Britain, he was an instant hit at the royal court. Everyone repeated his favorite French phrase "Ça ira" – "it'll be fine." Later it became the refrain of the revolutionary song "Ça ira" – an anthem of the French Revolution. The King and queen used family connections to secure Austrian and Russian support for the North American colonies against the British. Americans were so grateful that a town in Ohio was named after Marie Antoinette – Marietta! While helping Americans, Louis and his government paid no attention to the fact that revolutionary ideas were spreading like wildfire in France – even at the royal court itself. It wasn't too late: They could have woven their own narrative, opposing the revolution, and could have gone ahead with political reforms. They didn't. Like other European royals they were scared of being ridiculed and didn't dare to argue with the revolutionary intellectuals who controlled public opinion.

Marie Antoinette built a theater at the Petit Trianon where she performed in amateur musicals. She led a 'revolution' in fashion: A lighter, more natural makeup replaced layers of powder and blush. Instead of corsets and skirts mounted on hoops, the queen now wore a flowing multi-layer silk dress with a belt. Marie Antoinette's portrait painted by Madame Le Brun featured her new look and caused a scandal in the European fashion world.

Fashion evolution: Marie Antoinette portraits by Louise Élisabeth Vigée Le Brun; Left: Marie Antoinette's drawer chest

By 1781 Louis and Marie Antoinette had a son and a daughter.

While the royal court dealt with fashion scandals, the revolutionaries intensified their attacks on the royals. They distributed pamphlets describing their lavish lifestyle, banquets, masked balls, and love of gambling. Actually, many Parisians had a chance to glimpse the life of the royal court and see for themselves what was going on there. The vast gardens of Versailles were open to the public. Thousands came to see the King and Queen eat dinners outside the Petit Trianon. Louis XVI gobbled down many courses of artfully presented dishes and drank huge quantities of wine. Marie Antoinette drank only water, and hardly ate anything. Street vendors were allowed on the steps of the palace where they sold cocoa, coffee, and gingerbread to the crowds of visitors.

Rousseau had popularized the idea of being 'close to nature' (like 'noble savages'!) and living in the countryside. So aristocrats created fake 'villages' on their estates where they held 'rustic' retreats. Marie Antoinette built her own 'village' at Trianon – with 'farm houses,' a barn with farm animals, tiny streams, bridges, and a fake mill. Marie and her friends dressed as farm girls,

Marie Antoinette's bedroom in the Versailles Palace

ate strawberries in flower-decorated gazebos and played at making butter. Revolutionary activists had a lot to say about that. They even held it against her that she had accumulated a library of 5.000 books – mostly on music and history, the two subjects she was interested in. She was present at the launch of the Montgolfière – the world's first hot air balloon. That was condemned too, as another form of wasteful entertainment. In the streets, hatred of Marie Antoinette neared the boiling point, but the royals thought all that gossip in the newspapers was just the usual, common people's curiosity about celebrities.

French adventurer and writer Beaumarchais, who had helped the Louis XVI government to secretly arm American colonists, wrote a play *Marriage of Figaro* (a sequel to his previous work, *The Barber of Seville*). The play contained devastating satire of the French royal court, and Louis XVI banned it. Marie Antoinette, however, wanted to play a liberal patron of the arts and in 1784 the play debuted at the Theatre Francais. It was a smashing success because of the scorching sarcasm Beaumarchais directed at the ruling classes. Fearing the situation was getting out of hand, the king ordered Beaumarchais' arrest. He wrote his order on a playing card, since he was at the gambling table when that brilliant idea visited him. However, after a few days, the royals backed off, and the playwright was released – more popular than ever. Mozart wrote an opera based on the *Marriage of Figaro*, and Beaumarchais wrote pamphlets about the horrific conditions in French prisons and trials behind closed doors...Louis XVI had to apologize, paid some money to Beaumarchais, and ordered his government officials to attend the *Marriage of Figaro* at the Theatre Francais.

Belvédère at the Petit Trianon Palace; LouisXVI-era porcelain

Now revolutionaries knew for sure that Louis was a clueless weakling. Open contempt for the monarchy became a must in the salons of Paris.

The next scandal – the so-called 'Diamond Necklace Affair' – was even worse. King Louis XV ordered a diamond necklace to be designed for his favorite, Madame du Barry. The necklace was completed, but Louis XV died, never paying for it. That almost ruined the jewelers who had purchased extremely expensive diamonds for the necklace. Louis XVI, offered to buy it for Marie Antoinette, but she refused, because she hated Madame du Barry. In 1785 a female French *con artist* (a criminal using 'confidence'/persuasion tricks) Madame de la Motte convinced an aristocratic Cardinal of the Catholic Church – Cardinal de Rohan – that Marie Antoinette wanted the necklace, but wished to buy it secretly. De Rohan wanted a government appointment, and was eager to help. Madame de la Motte wrote letters to the Cardinal, telling him they were written by Marie Antoinette who was in love with him. Cardinal asked to see the Queen, and Madame de la Motte found a woman whose looks resembled Marie Antoinette, and paid her to pretend she was the queen in a dark corner of Versailles gardens where de Rohan came to see her. After that the Cardinal bought the necklace from the jewelers. The necklace was handed to the queen's 'messenger' (actually Madame de la Motte's accomplice). Within hours it was taken apart, and the diamonds were sold on the black markets of Paris and London.

Somehow the trick was exposed, and the Cardinal and Madame de la Motte were arrested. A scandalous trial followed. During the trial the cost of the necklace and many details of the corruption in the government became public knowledge. De Rohan was acquitted. De la Motte was sentenced to whipping, branding (the letter V for 'voleuse' – thief – was burned into her shoulders), and to imprisonment. In no time, however, she escaped from prison dressed as a boy, went to London, and published her 'version' of the story, accusing Marie Antoinette of deception and greed. The British made sure these accusations reached the salons in Paris and the hatred for Marie Antoinette flared up higher than ever.

A copy of Madam du Barry's necklace

As the onset of the revolution approached, the poverty in France was at its worst, and the treasury was empty. Louis was now suffering from depression, and Marie Antoinette got involved in politics. She appointed a new Minister of Finance, De Calonne, famous for his promise to the queen: "Madame, if it's possible, it'll be done, and if it's impossible, it'll still be done."

De Calonne failed to replenish the treasury, and in January of 1787 the king was forced to announce elections to the General Assembly – to get his subjects to agree to raise taxes even higher. At the Assembly, after Louis XVI finished his speech, he put on his hat. The noblemen put on their hats too, according to the custom. Then, suddenly, the Third Estate – the deputies of the people – put on their hats as well. That was against the rules! It was a gesture that challenged the privileges of the upper classes – the first demand for equality. Aristocrats shouted "Hats off!" but the people's deputies didn't move. Silence descended on the assembly hall. Louis was the first to cave in. Terrified of open confrontation, he took off his hat. Then everybody took off their hats, and everybody knew: Louis had just let go of that royal authority for which his ancestors killed and died in battles.

On the eve of the revolution, a month before the storming of the Bastille, the royal family suffered an enormous loss – the king's eldest son died of tuberculosis at age 7. Normally this would have been a major event, but, as the clouds of the revolution gathered and the royal family was hated or scorned by so many, nobody seemed to notice.

Louis XVI agrees to wear a liberty cap and drink to the health of the French Republic

After the Women's March the royal family moved into the abandoned Tuileries (tu-il-ree) Palace in Paris where they lived as prisoners. Arriving at Tuileries, the first thing Louis did was ask for a history book on the trial and execution of Charles I of England. That was telling. Printed reports of Charles I's trial were sold on every corner in Paris. Revolutionary agitators made the crowds wild with the question,"If the English put their king to death and have become a free nation, why won't we do the same?"

With no hunting and no court, both Louis and Marie Antoinette were depressed and often sick. They didn't dare to leave the palace under the watch of Lafayette's National Guard. Finally, a loyal friend, Count Fersen, arranged for them to escape. He smuggled in clothes for them to use as a disguise. The king would dress as a servant, and the queen as a governess (tutor and baby-sitter) to her two kids. Marie Antoinette's second son, who was 6, would be dressed as a girl. The royal family left the palace in the middle of the night, but on the road a delay happened: The horses stumbled and broke the harness. It took forever to fix it. They missed the carriage that expected them at one of their stops, and, finally, along the way, the king was recognized by a postmaster who sympathized with the revolutionaries.

The spot in Varennes where the royal family was captured

When the royal family reached Varennes in north-eastern France, soldiers of the revolutionary guard dispatched by Lafayette were already waiting for them. The royals were locked in a room above a local grocery shop.

"Capture in Varennes" by Thomas Falcon Marshall

One of the king's supporters secretly made his way into the room and asked for orders. To the shock of this man, risking his life for his king, Louis responded, "I am a prisoner: I have no orders to give." On the way back to Paris crowds followed the royal carriage, demanding the heads of the king, the queen, and even of Lafayette, who had failed to secure the royal prisoners in the Tuileries. The next day Paris echoed the words Danton addressed to Lafayette: "France can be free without you."

Lafayette's revolutionary career ended in 1791 with the Champ de Mars massacre. He arrived to restore order on the Champ de Mars ('Field of Mars' in French) – a park in Paris where crowds assembled demanding the abolition of the monarchy. The rioters had already engaged in violence, having hung two men (supposedly royalist spies) on the lampposts. The rebels threw stones at Lafayette and fired at him. In return, Lafayette ordered the National Guard to fire at the crowd. Calling for Lafayette's trial and execution the next day, Marat claimed that over 400 citizens of Paris had been killed by Lafayette and dumped into the river. Lafayette's house was attacked by the sans-culottes, and he had to leave Paris.

Back at the Tuileries the royal family were now prisoners for real. Guards now stood in every room and hallway. In June 1792, a mob of sans-culottes attacked the Tuileries, and, singing *Ca Ira*, broke into the palace. Instead of banners, they were carrying sticks with pants tied to them – the symbol of the sans-culottes – and a doll hanging by its neck on a stick and labeled 'Marie Antoinette.' They made the king wear the red 'liberty cap' and drink wine 'to the health of the Republic.'

Revolutionary crowds break into the Tuileries

"The Swiss Guard massacre" by Jacques Bertaux

During this raid a young officer of the revolutionary army, who watched on from a street corner nearby, asked his comrade, "Why have the royal guards let the mob into the palace? The guards should've erased 400-500 of them with a cannon. The rest would've run away fast enough." That was the future emperor of France, Napoleon Bonaparte. He despised Louis XVI as an ultimate loser. "If he had just mounted his horse, the victory would have been his," Napoleon commented years later.

Two months after the Tuileries sans-culottes attack, revolutionary troops from Marseilles, singing the *Marseillaise*, marched into Paris, supposedly to help maintain order. Instead, they headed straight to the Tuileries Palace. This time, the palace had a cannon, plus 800 royal Swiss guards and 1200 nobles ready to defend the king. Louis XVI, however, was scared, again, and didn't dare to put the cannon in action. Instead, together with his family, he ran out through a garden gate, leaving his supporters to defend an empty palace. Nearly all of them perished.

Napoleon Bonaparte at 23 by Henri Félix Emmanuel Philippoteaux

Revolutionaries then went house-to-house arresting 'suspects.' Hundreds of priests and aristocrats were thrown in jail or killed in the streets. Even more fled France. The country was now in the hands of three men – Marat, Danton, and Robespierre, and they promised their followers the king's head. Bit by bit, revolutionaries stripped Louis of any remnants of his authority. They accompanied this process with symbolic gestures designed to crush the king's spirit – such as taking away his sword and his orders of knighthood. Then he was separated from his wife and kids, and finally accused of treason and placed on trial.

At the trial he was referred to not as the former king, but as 'Louis Capet' – Capet being the name of the French royal dynasty tracing itself to Charlemagne. Louis certainly knew that the trial was nothing but a fake justification of his murder. "They will bring me to the scaffold," he told his lawyer, "but I will eventually win if I leave an unspotted memory behind me." When the king was declared 'guilty,' the Convention voted to have Louis guillotined within 24 hours.

The trial of Louis XVI

Thomas Paine, one of the leaders of the American Revolution who at that time lived in Paris, protested, saying, "The man whom you condemn to death is regarded by the people of the United States as their best friend, as the founder of liberty!" Given an honorary French citizenship and elected to the Convention, Paine argued that his country was grateful to Louis for supporting the American Revolution and proposed that the king be exiled to the United States. Paine didn't speak French, he addressed the Convention through an interpreter. Afraid that his speech could reverse the death sentence, Marat interrupted Thomas Paine and accused his interpreter of distorting Paine's words. Indignant, Paine provided a written version of his speech, but it was too late.

The king was allowed to say goodbye to Marie Antoinette and his children, and asked his son, the dauphin, not to avenge his death. On the day of his execution the streets of Paris were lined with troops, and the city was absolutely silent. Many thought that the murder of the king would be punished by God. On the scaffold erected in the middle of the Place de la Revolution (the 'Square of the Revolution' – now the Place de la Concorde – the 'Square of Peace'), before beheading, Louis addressed the crowd, saying, "I die innocent of the crimes they accused me of. I forgive those who sentenced me to death, and I pray that my blood may not fall upon France..." But the commander of the guard didn't let him continue. He ordered the drums to be beaten to drown Louis' speech. At the moment of the execution an abbot who was allowed to accompany the king exclaimed "Son of Saint Louis, ascend to heaven!" When the executioner showed the crowd Louis's head, there was silence. Then everyone shouted "Vive la Republique!" – 'Long live the Republic!' And that was the end of the **Ancien Régime** (French for 'Old Regime') as they now referred to the French monarchy.
King Louis XVI was 38 when he died.

Soon Marie Antoinette was accused of treason. Her trial was short. When ordered to give the names of other "traitors who plotted against the nation," she answered, "I shall never testify against my subjects. I have seen all, understood all, and forgotten all." To crush Marie's spirit, the accusers announced that one of her kids, the dauphin, had accused her of teaching him inappropriate things. "I appeal to every mother here present, whether such a thing is possible!" responded Marie Antoinette. The spectators in the courtroom burst into applause. Concerned that she could win the sympathy of the people, the revolutionaries wrapped up the trial, at the end of which the queen said, "I was a queen and you took away my crown...a wife, and you murdered my husband...a mother, and you robbed me of my children. My blood alone remains. Take it, but do not make me suffer long."

In prison Marie Antoinette wrote a letter to her sister-in-law, in which she forgave all her enemies, and asked her children never to try to avenge her death. The letter was snatched from Marie Antoinette by the guards and later found among the papers of the judge who had sentenced her. His apartment was searched when he was arrested by his former revolutionary comrades, right before he, too, was taken to the guillotine – in the same creaky old cart that had carried Marie Antoinette to her death.

"Marie Antoinette and her children" by Elisabeth Louise Vigée Le Brun, "Painter Jacques-Louis David drawing Marie-Antoinette led to her execution" by Joseph-Emmanuel van den Bussche. Below: Jacques-Louis David's actual drawing of Marie Antoinette being taken to the guillotine. A deputy of the Convention, and a member of the Jacobin Club, David voted for her death.

NAPOLEON
1769 – 1821

10 years after it began, having taken over 40,000 lives, the French Revolution fizzled out. Military disasters and riots shook France. The Directory – yet another revolutionary government – was overthrown and replaced by three 'consuls,' including Napoleon Bonaparte. Napoleon was born on the Italian island of Corsica in the Mediterranean Sea, in 1769 – the year the island was conquered by France. His native language was Italian, so when at age 9 he was sent to a military school in France, French kids bullied him for his Italian accent calling him a 'peasant.' This only increased Napoleon's hatred for the French – the 'occupiers' of Corsica.

Napoleon's dad was an attorney, both parents were from noble families. They had 9 kids, of whom Napoleon was to become an emperor, while 3 of his brothers were to become kings, and the three sisters – a queen and 2 princesses. Napoleon's favorite book was, not surprisingly, Plutarch's *Lives of the Noble Greeks and Romans*, and his second favorite was Julius Cæsar's *Gallic Wars*. At 15 Napoleon was sent to a military academy in Paris, where his classmates nicknamed him 'Spartan' because of his simple tastes. Meanwhile Napoleon was stunned by the luxury and wastefulness of the wealthy Parisians and the royal court.

Napoleon's coronation portrait by Francois Gerard

When the revolution started, Napoleon became a supporter of Robespierre and the Jacobins. He commanded artillery in a few military campaigns of the revolutionary government, and was quite successful until the fall of Robespierre and the Jacobins when his career went into a downward spiral. At this point Napoleon was not sure what to do. He considered serving the Turkish sultan in Istanbul and even wrote a novel about a revolutionary soldier who is betrayed by the woman he loves. Then, in 1795 royalists staged a rebellion in Paris, and the revolutionaries needed urgent help defending the Convention (revolutionary government) besieged in the Tuileries Palace. Napoleon, who had seen the massacre of the Swiss Guards in front of the Tuileries 3 years earlier, did exactly what Louis XVI should have done – he ordered a massive artillery attack on the royalists. Over 1,400 of the rebels perished and the rest fled. A new revolutionary government, the 5-member committee called the Directory replaced the National Convention.

Now Napoleon was famous and appointed commander of whole armies. He also met and married Joséphine de Beauharnais, a widow with two kids, whose husband had been guillotined by the revolutionaries. Josephine grew up in the French West Indies. She was charming and Napoleon said about her, "I win battles, but Josephine wins hearts!" During this period Napoleon led successful French campaigns against Austria and Italy, his military strategy inspired by detailed study of battles won by Hannibal, Alexander the Great, and Julius Caesar. His influence in Paris deepened, and some politicians warned that Napoleon, just like Caesar, was aiming at taking control of his country as a dictator. Napoleon's military plans now included the invasion of Britain, Egypt, and India. His famous phrase "Imagination rules the world" described his large-scale strategy: If he could imagine it, he would take a risk and try it.

Joséphine de Beauharnais

IS IT TRUE THAT NAPOLEON WAS SHORT?

Many cartoons of his era portray Napoleon as short and round, wearing ridiculously large hats and boots. Actually he was 5'7" – taller than the average man of his time. Napoleon cared about being portrayed in a heroic light, so his enemies, especially the British, did exactly the opposite, making him look ridiculous. When Britain declared war on France in 1803, Napoleon ordered the arrest and imprisonment of every British citizen found anywhere in French territories. Any ship that stopped at a British port, even briefly, was ordered to be captured. That's when the British anti-Napoleon propaganda kicked into high gear.

On the Egyptian campaign Napoleon brought with him 167 French scientists and engineers to study the heritage of Ancient Egypt and bring back Egyptian treasures as trophies. Among other discoveries, they found the Rosetta Stone bearing an inscription in 3 languages – Egyptian hieroglyphs, Egyptian Demotic script, and Greek. The inscription dated to 196 BC and enabled scholars to decipher the ancient Egyptian language. Wherever Napoleon went, he carried with him his 'traveling library' – two trunks with bookshelves inside. Sailing to Egypt, on the ship, Napoleon read the *Voyages of Captain Cook* and listened to discussions among the scientists. Once, pointing at the stars, he told them, "You may talk as long as you please, gentlemen, but who made all that?"

With 25,000 troops, Napoleon succeeded in conquering Egypt, ruled by **Mamluks**. Mamluks were mercenaries and slave-soldiers who came from the steppes of Southern Russia and the Caucasus mountains in the Middle Ages and served Arab and Turkish Muslim sultans. Eventually they ended up ruling some areas on their own. Landing in Alexandria, Napoleon captured the fort, promised the local Arabs to free them from Mamluks and ordered them to start building factories and schools. He did everything to appeal to the local inhabitants: ate Arab lentil soup, took part in the Nile festival, and even showed up wearing native Arab clothes. During the march south, to Cairo, Napoleon walked at the head of his troops – for 60 miles on foot across burning sand – sharing all the hardships with ordinary soldiers. Whenever any signs of danger appeared, French commanders gave an order, "Form square! Donkeys and scientists to the center!" Donkeys and scientists were equally useless when it came to fighting.

"Bonaparte in front of the Sphynx" by Jean Leon Gerome

Before the famous Battle of the Pyramids fought near the great pyramids of Giza, Napoleon addressed his troops with the words, "Soldiers, from the summits of these pyramids 40 centuries are looking down upon you!" In that battle the Mamluks lost over 2 thousand fighters, while the French lost only 29 men. Then a setback occurred: On August 1, 1798, the British Navy led by Admiral Nelson destroyed the French fleet – along with Napoleon's plans to conquer India. Napoleon needed more victories to compensate for this disaster. His army swept along the Mediterranean coast, taking Arab towns of Gaza, Jaffa, and Haifa (on the territory of modern Israel). In Jaffa he ordered 2000 prisoners of war to be executed by drowning and allowed his troops to plunder the city for 3 days. On the way back to Egypt Napoleon's army was struck by plague. Thousands of his soldiers died. To lift up the spirits of his troops, Napoleon visited the sick, but the Mamluk army was following him, and the sick were a burden. Napoleon asked the chief doctor of the French army to poison the sick soldiers with opium, but the doctor stayed true to his Hippocratic Oath. "My art teaches me to cure men, not to kill them," he responded. This didn't stop Napoleon, and hundreds of French soldiers were killed by poison.

In 1799, when Napoleon returned to Paris, he realized that the Directory had lost popular support and organized a **coup d'état** (a government overthrow, literally 'strike of the state' in French). The revolutionary deputies knew what he was up to. Their Council of Five Hundred met Napoleon with shouts "Down with the tyrant! No Cromwell! Down with the Dictator! Outlaw him!" But Napoleon commanded the army, it was best not to argue with him. The Directory, committee of 5, was replaced by a committee of 3 'consuls' (in a reference to the consuls of Ancient Rome) headed by Napoleon.

"General Bonaparte in the Council of Five Hundred" by Francois Bouchot

"The coronation of Napoleon" by Jacques-Louis David

The history of Ancient Rome taught Napoleon that the magic word 'democracy' could make any regime look respectable, so he organized an 'elections theater.' Citizens of France were invited to vote in a **plebiscite** (direct vote of the people, from the Latin *plēbs* – common people, plebeians) for a new constitution that secured Napoleon's position as the First Consul. The elections were rigged (falsified) by Napoleon's brother, Lucien Bonaparte. The results showed that 3 million people voted (actually only 1.5 million) and that 99.94% voted for Napoleon's constitution. Right away Napoleon moved into the Tuileries Palace with Josephine and her family. Noticing worn-out tricolor banners and 'liberty caps' on spikes decorating the palace, Napoleon ordered, "Remove this garbage." That was the end of the French Revolution.

"Conquest has made me what I am, and conquest alone can maintain me." Following this conclusion, Napoleon ordered his troops to cross the Swiss Alps into Italy to surprise the Austrian army deployed there. He dreamed of repeating the crossing of the Alps by the great hero of ancient Carthage, Hannibal. To the objections of his generals he responded "*Impossible* is not a French word." Passing through Geneva, Napoleon visited the burial place of Rousseau. Standing by Rousseau's grave, he shocked his companions with the following observation: "Well, the future must decide whether the world would have been happier had neither I nor Rousseau ever lived."

Napoleon survived a few assassination attempts and, in 1804, he used them to justify giving himself the powers of an emperor – following the model of the Roman Empire. To portray himself an 'heir' of Charlemagne who was crowned by a pope, Napoleon invited Pope Pius VII to the coronation ceremony at Notre Dame. A golden chariot drawn by 8 white horses brought Napoleon to the coronation. He wore a white silk robe and a velvet mantle lined with ermine and weighing 80 pounds – all embroidered with golden bees. He had a golden wreath on his head like those worn by Roman emperors. Suddenly, in the crowd of guests, he noticed an acquaintance – a lawyer, who, years ago, had advised Josephine against marrying Napoleon, because he was poor. "He has nothing but a soldier's sword and cape," the lawyer had said about the young military commander. Napoleon never forgot that. Right there, at the coronation, he approached the man, and, pointing at his royal mantle and the sword decorated with massive gems, asked, "See the soldier's sword and cape?"

Napoleon refused to be crowned by anyone, including the Pope, and placed the crown on his own head.

A portrait of Napoleon by Jacques-Louis David

THE BEE

The bee was the emblem of the Merovingian dynasty of the kings of the Franks, who ruled the territory of present-day France during the Dark Ages, following the collapse of the Roman Empire. Chosen by Napoleon as an emblem of his dynasty, the bee was considered a symbol of immortality and hard work.

SOME WEIRD HABITS OF NAPOLEON & JOSEPHINE

Napoleon was afraid of open doors. All doors had to be closed at all times, and if anyone entered the room where Napoleon was sitting, they had to open the door just a little, squeeze through quickly, and immediately shut the door behind them. Napoleon's favorite food was roasted chicken with fried potatoes and onions. He loved playing cards and always cheated. He slept only 3-4 hours a night. While Marie-Antoinette bought about 170 dresses a year, Napoleon's wife Josephine bought 900 dresses a year and 1000 pairs of gloves!

"Napoleon meets Russian colonel Prince Repnin-Volkonsky, captured at the battle of Austerlitz" by Francois Gerard

In 1805 Britain, Russia, Austria, and Sweden joined in a coalition against Napoleon. But Napoleon, with his La Grande Armée – the Great Army, outwitted and defeated the Austrian army. He took Vienna, the capital of Austria, then destroyed the joint Austrian-Russian forces in the Battle of Austerlitz. Next, Prussia (Northern Germany) was also defeated, and now Napoleon was marching across Poland toward Russia. Poland didn't exist as a state at that time. Its territory was divided between Austria, Prussia, and Russia. Its former capital, Warsaw, was in Prussia. The Polish nobility hoped Napoleon would liberate Poland and restore its independence. They convinced a young Polish noblewoman, Marie Walewska, to try to charm Napoleon. Sure enough, he fell in love with her and they started dating. However, Napoleon viewed Poland as nothing but swampy borderlands between France and Russia. He liked Russian Emperor Alexander I and wanted a 'deal' with the Russians.

"Marie Walewska" by Francois Gerard

In 1807 Napoleon and Alexander met on a raft anchored in the middle of the Nieman River on the Russian border, and signed a treaty that effectively divided continental Europe between the two of them. The only item they couldn't agree upon was Constantinople. Each wanted it for his own empire. Napoleon was flattered by Alexander's friendliness and gave him lavish gifts. In return, Alexander shared with Napoleon Russian-made maps valuable for exploration and war.

This deal was a disaster for Poland. Marie Walewska's personal hopes were shattered as well. She and Napoleon had a baby, but just before the baby was born, Napoleon divorced Josephine and married Marie-Louise, daughter of the Austrian emperor Francis II and a grand niece of Marie-Antoinette. He claimed that, since he and Josephine didn't have children, he needed a new marriage that would give him kids. So why not Marie Walewska who had a baby with him? Because what Napoleon really needed was to marry into European royalty. He had actually proposed to a Russian princess first, but, getting no positive response, went after Marie-Louise. Marie-Louise wasn't thrilled to marry him either. They quoted her saying, "Just seeing this man would be the worst form of torture." Napoleon had doubts as well. He believed in fate and felt that having abandoned Josephine he lost his luck. Later he even called his second marriage "that abyss covered with flowers that was my ruin." Napoleon's friends and supporters were also shocked. Everyone knew that Josephine's intelligence and charm had contributed a lot to Napoleon's success. "He divorced his guardian angel," they said in the streets of Paris. Nevertheless, Napoleon and Marie-Louise made the marriage work and had a son.

Napoleon meets Tsar Alexander on a raft in the middle of the Nieman River

"Empress Josephine signs her divorce agreement" by Henry Frederic Schopin
"Marriage of Napoleon and Marie-Louise" by Georges Rouget

The official announcement of their child's gender was arranged to be twenty-one gun shots for a daughter and one hundred for a son. Thousands outside the Tuileries counted the shots until it became clear that the Emperor had a son, the much-expected heir to his throne.

Meanwhile, clouds were gathering in the East. Russian Emperor Alexander stopped playing nice and – behind Napoleon's back – was negotiating with Napoleon's Minister of Foreign Affairs Talleyrand. Talleyrand disagreed with Napoleon's famous statement that "God is on the side of the biggest battalions." Talleyrand believed Napoleon was talentless as a political thinker, and that one day he would destroy his own empire. And that day was fast approaching.

In 1811 Napoleon raised the "army of twenty nations" – nearly 680 thousand to invade Russia. His troops came not only from France, but from all across Europe – there were German, Italian, Dutch, Austrian, Swiss, Spanish, and Portuguese soldiers. To get the Polish to join his army, Napoleon called his Russian campaign the 'Polish War,' promising to liberate the Polish lands held by Russia. 85 thousand Poles joined his army. Among the French, however, there was no enthusiasm for invading Russia. At least 80 thousand French soldiers deserted Napoleon's army before the Russian campaign. The Russian army was much smaller – only 400 thousand troops, but there was something about the idea of invading Russia that didn't feel quite right. Over the maps, where Russia stretched from its borders with Germany all the way to the Pacific and beyond, into Alaska, Napoleon's generals attempted to talk him out of his plans. He ignored them. "The Emperor is insane, quite insane," wrote Admiral Decres, the commander of the French Navy, to a friend. "He will ruin us all, many as we are, and everything will end in a horrific catastrophe."

In June 1812 Napoleon's army crossed the Nieman River into Russia. French officer, Captain Eugene Labaume wrote in his memoir: "As we reached the opposite shore, it seemed to us that even the air there was different. The roads were horrible, the forests dark and gloomy, and the villages completely deserted. But our imagination, inflamed by a spirit of conquest, was enchanted with everything, and cherished illusions which were soon destroyed."

The first weeks in Russia were promising. Napoleon's army entered Vilna (present-day Vilnius), capital of Lithuania, which at that time was in the Russian Empire. Russians evacuated their garrison and left without any resistance. It was suspicious, but nobody gave it much thought because there was a big party ahead! Lithuania had been disputed between Poland and Russia.

The Polish supporters of Napoleon expected him to give Lithuania to Poland and organized a big celebration presenting Vilna as a Polish town. They handed Napoleon the keys to Vilna and wore national Polish costumes at lavish banquets and receptions in his honor. In the following weeks the Russian army, led by commander-in-chief Mikhail Kutuzov, kept retreating, putting up only occasional resistance. Russians evacuated towns and villages and burned everything behind them – fields, farms, and city buildings. Entering empty, ruined settlements, Napoleon's army had problems feeding and supplying the troops. Napoleon was worried. "Russia is too powerful to yield without fighting," he told his generals, "Tsar Alexander will not negotiate until he fights and loses in a great battle."

Napoleon was a brilliant battle strategist. Russians knew this and, instead of meeting him in a battle, sought to wear the French army out and trap it. The biggest battle they fought against Napoleon – the 'great battle' he was looking forward to – was the Battle of Borodino near Moscow, and the Russians lost it. 30 thousand Russian and 40 thousand French soldiers perished. Years later Napoleon wrote about it, "The most terrible of all my battles was the one before Moscow. The French showed themselves to be worthy of victory, but the Russians showed themselves worthy of being invincible." Then strange things started happening...

"Napoleon watches Moscow burn" by Adam Albrecht

Napoleon sent the units of his guard to Moscow to prepare for his triumphal entry. His men, however, reported that Russians had evacuated nearly all the quarter million of Moscow's inhabitants and there was nobody to greet him. As Napoleon rode through the streets of Moscow the following day, they were empty except for beggars and convicts released from prisons. Then, suddenly, gunpowder cellars started exploding all over the city. On the order of the Moscow governor, count Rastopchin, the city was set on fire. The fire raged for 3 days, burning 9/10 of Moscow down to the ground.

Napoleon expected Tsar Alexander to negotiate the surrender, but there was no word from the tsar. The capital of Russia wasn't Moscow. It was St.Petersburg – way in the North, far off the path of Napoleon's army. Moscow could be sacrificed. After 5 weeks in the smoking ruins of Moscow, Napoleon got it: He was trapped in the vastness of Russia and Russians were in no hurry to negotiate or even attack. They were waiting for their best ally – winter. In a moment of panic Napoleon reached out to Tsar Alexander offering him Constantinople if he agreed to negotiate. Alexander was amused. "I would rather dig potatoes in Siberia than negotiate while the enemy is on Russian soil," he commented.

Another miscalculation haunted Napoleon. He expected Russians to greet him as a liberator, the way he was welcomed in Poland. The poverty and oppression of the working people in Russia were as savage as in France under monarchy. Instead, common Russians, including the poorest of the poor, unleashed a brutal guerilla war on Napoleon's troops, as the rising wave of patriotism united all classes of Russian society. The winter came early that year. Napoleon's army was not prepared or equipped for -20C (-4F), common in Russia in November. Napoleon gave an order to retreat back to Poland, and as his 'march of humiliation' began, the Russians started to attack.

NAPOLEON'S TREASURE

Retreating from Moscow, Napoleon carried with him a huge load of gold and silver plundered in the Kremlin. As Russian attacks intensified, Napoleon ordered the treasure buried. His officers' memoirs say it was sunk in a lake. Russian treasure hunters are still looking for it!

"French troops retreating from Moscow" by I.M. Prianishnikov

Napoleon's soldiers were carrying large amounts of plunder collected in Moscow. That, and the knee-deep snow on the roads, slowed their march down to a crawl. Suddenly, the temperatures dropped below -30C (-22F). Over 10 thousand of Napoleon's soldiers froze to death, and many died of starvation and disease. Captain Labaume recalled that "no dead horse or cattle remained uneaten, no dog, no cat, nor even the corpses of those who died of cold and hunger... Our soldiers, struggling with the blizzard, could no longer distinguish the road, and many, falling into the ditches, found a grave there. Others pressed on, scarcely able to drag themselves along. They were badly clothed, with nothing to eat or drink, shaking from the cold, and groaning with pain....They hardly even looked at those who fell down and died, exhausted by fatigue and disease. Packs of dogs followed us from Moscow, feeding on the remains of our soldiers. They kept howling around us, waiting for us to become their prey."

It took Napoleon's army 2 months to get out of Russia. During the crossing of the Berezina River (in Belorussia) the French troops were ambushed. They worked all night building pontoon bridges, up to their necks in water, struggling with ice carried down by the swift current. In the morning, as they were crossing the river, Russians attacked. Escaping, the French troops rushed onto the bridges. The bridges collapsed, hurling thousands into the icy waters.

"Napoleon's retreat from Moscow" by Adolph Northen

The next day Russians collected and burned on the banks of the river 30 thousand dead bodies of Napoleon's men. Of the 680 thousand soldiers that marched into Russia, less than 20 thousand crossed Berezina and came home. And what did Napoleon have to say about this? "I grew up in the field, and a man like me troubles himself little about the lives of a million of men," he explained later. Before the remnants of the "army of twenty nations" reached Vilna, Napoleon abandoned his troops and left for Paris. He said he was concerned about a conspiracy back home, but many believed he was tortured by the memories of all those celebrations the Polish had held in Vilna in his honor. When Napoleon's Polish supporters asked him to keep his promise and liberate Poland, they were explained that by "liberating" the emperor didn't mean making Poland independent. He had already promised Poland to Austria.

Above: "Berezina" by Peter von Hess; Below:"Retreat from Moscow" by Pjotr C. Stojanow

Tsar Alexander and Russian troops enter Paris

The following year the European allies joined forces with Russia and defeated Napoleon's army in Europe. In March 1814 Russian and allied troops marched into Paris. Tsar Alexander of Russia and Frederick William of Prussia rode side by side through the streets of Paris, while the crowds shouted demanding the restoration of French monarchy. They were done with the revolution and the empire. Napoleon tried to commit suicide by poison he always wore in a bag on a cord around his neck. But the poison had lost its potency, and he survived. Napoleon was exiled to Elba, a small island in the Mediterranean where he was allowed to be a ruler and retain the title of an Emperor. This 'sentence' was an act of mockery, of course. The island is about 12x17 sq. miles and had an 'army' of 400 soldiers. Empress Marie Louise refused to join Napoleon on Elba, returned to Vienna, and never saw him again. In France monarchy was restored and the brother of King Louis XVI was crowned king Louis XVIII. He promptly moved into the Tuileries Palace and ordered every single bee (Napoleon's emblem) on the walls and on the banners be turned into a ***fleur-de-lis*** (lily flower), the symbol of the Bourbon royal dynasty. Louis XVIII was petty, vengeful, and unpopular even among the royalists. Speaking of him, Napoleon said, "The Bourbons have learned nothing and have forgotten nothing."

On Elba, Napoleon created a small army and started developing iron mines to eventually manufacture weapons. In February of 1815, with 700 loyal supporters, he escaped from Elba and came ashore in France. A regiment of soldiers was sent to capture Napoleon near Grenoble, but Napoleon rode to meet the French soldiers alone, and when he approached them, he got off his horse and shouted, "Here I am. Kill your Emperor, if you wish." Napoleon walked toward the soldiers, looking in their faces. Suddenly he recognized a few of them and called them by name. Stunned, the soldiers responded with, "Vive L'Empereur!" ('Long live the Emperor!') and took Napoleon's side. More and more troops loyal to Napoleon joined his new army, as Napoleon marched toward Paris. Louis XVIII escaped to Austria and Napoleon entered Paris and ruled there for the period known as the 'Hundred Days.'

"Napoleon's return from Elba" by Charles de Steuben

In June 1815 the coalition of Great Britain, Russia, Austria, and Prussia defeated Napoleon in the Battle of Waterloo, Netherlands (present-day Belgium). He tried to board a ship to escape to the United States, but the British Navy blocked every French port, and Napoleon surrendered. He was taken to Plymouth, England, aboard the British Navy ship Bellerophon. The ship was docked at Plymouth for 2 weeks, and every day, hundreds of people came to the harbor hoping to see Napoleon. Flattered by this 'celebrity worship,' Napoleon appeared on the deck every day at 6:30 pm and even waved to his English fans. Then Napoleon was informed he would be exiled to the island of Saint Helena in the Atlantic Ocean off the west coast of Africa. When he protested, they told him, "Better St. Helena than Russia." "God keep me from that," Napoleon answered quickly.

On St. Helena Napoleon lived with a group of friends. Josephine had died, Marie Louise and her son were in Austria. He dictated his memoirs, wrote a book about Julius Caesar, studied English, and demanded that his friends appeared at dinner wearing military uniforms and their wives wearing evening gowns and jewelry. He fell ill, and there was a suspicion of slow poisoning by arsenic. Napoleon died in 1821 at age 51. The last word he pronounced was "Josephine."

"Napoleon on the Arcole Bridge, 1796" by Antoine Jean Gros & "Abdication of Napoleon, 1815" by Paul Delaroche

Artists, writers, actors, journalists, and other people of creative talent have always been recruited by political movements & leaders to engage in what we now call 'propaganda" – the promotion and glorification of political goals. Jacques-Louis David – a painter, whose creative career flourished during the decade of the French Revolution and the Napoleonic era – started as an active participant in the French revolutionary movement, and a believer in democracy. But he ended up serving Napoleon's empire-building dictatorship. David's style of art was *neoclassicism,* drawing inspiration from the art and history of ancient Greece and Rome. David was especially famous for his paintings illustrating the history of the Roman republic.

JACQUES-LOUIS DAVID
1748 – 1825

Jacques-Louis David grew up in a wealthy family. His first teacher was his distant relative and the star of the French *rococo* style, François Boucher. Rococo was a light-hearted and decorative style, featuring pastel colors, mythological characters, and a lot of floral motifs and golden swirls. But as the revolution approached, tastes were changing. The playfulness of rococo was going away. Like Marat, who was rejected by the French Academy of Sciences (and never forgave his more successful rivals), David clashed with the Royal Academy of Arts. As a 23-year-old student at the Academy, he sought a prestigious Academy prize that would pay for his study of art and architecture in Rome. He applied for this 3 times, but was never chosen. David put some pressure on his teachers by going on a hunger strike. He didn't eat for 2 days, and that may have helped. On the 4th attempt he was granted the prize, but his hatred for the Academy never left him.

Rococo: "A secret message" by David's teacher Francois Boucher

When David returned to Paris his star started rising. In 1781 he became a member of the Royal Academy, and Louis XVI gave him an apartment in the Louvre palace – a great honor. David married a daughter of the palace manager, and that brought him connections and money. When Louis XVI's government commissioned him a painting depicting a story from Roman history, David refused to accept unless he was paid to paint it in Rome, because "Only in Rome can I paint Romans." His father-in-law provided the money and David left for Rome where he painted *The Oath of the Horatii*, based on the legend of the three brothers of the Roman Horatii family going to fight three brothers from the enemy city Alba Longa to decide the outcome of a war. In the painting the three brothers make an oath to sacrifice their lives for the Roman republic, while their father holds their swords. According to Roman legend, after the battle only one brother survived.

A lesser-known part of the Horatii legend tells of Camilla, one of the Horatii sisters depicted in the right corner of David's painting. Camilla was secretly engaged to one of the three brothers from Alba Longa. When her fiance fell in the battle, she cried over his body. Seeing this, Camilla's surviving brother killed her for placing love above patriotism. There is no question that David interpreted the death of Camilla as appropriate punishment for weakness – equal to treason in time of war. Only a few years later, elected to the revolutionary government, David would send hundreds of 'traitors' to the guillotine. *The Oath of the Horatii* was his personal oath – the statement of how far he himself was prepared to go to make his revolutionary dreams a reality.

David's next big work, *The Death of Socrates*, was also infused with the spirit of the approaching revolution. Sentenced to death by poison (hemlock) for criticizing the government of ancient Athens, Socrates says goodbye to his friends and students. He dies for the freedom of speech. How is it possible that this powerful work was created by the man who – only a few years later – would send to the guillotine people who expressed a 'wrong' idea or voted for a 'wrong' political candidate? While Parisian intellectuals praised Jacques-Louis David for standing for free speech, his conflict with the Royal Academy deepened. The Academy refused to give him the job of its director in Rome, and *The Death of Socrates* didn't receive the Academy award David expected. Too bad for the Academy! The clock was ticking. It was 1787 – 2 years to the fall of the Bastille.

Just as the French Revolution erupted and the Bastille fell, David showed his new painting, *The Lictors Bring to Brutus the Bodies of His Sons* – at the Salon, the annual exhibition of the Royal Academy of Arts. The story depicted in this work continues the theme of Camilla – love, family, and friendship must be sacrificed to patriotism. Any personal weakness is equal to treason. Lucius Junius Brutus (6th century BC) was one of the first consuls of the Roman Republic. He sentenced to death his two sons for conspiring to bring back the Roman monarchy.

As the revolution went on, David quickly transformed from a sensitive artist and the self-proclaimed defender of liberty, to a ruthless and fanatical member of a tyrannical government. He made friends with Marat and Robespierre, joined the Jacobin Club, was elected to the National Convention, and voted for the execution of Louis XVI. David's wife, Marguerite Charlotte, a royalist, was disgusted with the 'bloodthirsty' attitude of her husband and divorced him over his vote. His Jacobin friends, however, appointed him to the Committee of Public Safety and gave him a telling nickname – 'ferocious terrorist.' Next, David went after the Royal Academy of Painting and Sculpture. In no time it was abolished. Terrified of David, artists called him 'the Robespierre of the brush' and 'the Raphael of the sans-culottes.'
But David couldn't care less what the artistic community thought of him. He didn't need the Academy's awards and grants anymore. At this point he viewed art as a propaganda tool, and for his own artistic work he was now paid directly by the revolutionary government.

The biggest painting David ever worked on was *The Tennis Court Oath*, portraying the deputies of the Third Estate gathering at the royal tennis court in June 1789 when they were locked out of the General Assembly meeting. This was the historical moment when the deputies of the people proclaimed themselves the revolutionary National Assembly. In 1789 this event was regarded as the heroic peak of the revolution... However, 2-3 years later, when David started working on *The Tennis Court Oath*, many of the participants of that event were no longer 'heroes.' They had been sent to the guillotine as traitors. Some had been sentenced by David himself... So our artist had to abandon his project.

When Marat was assassinated by Charlotte Corday, David was given the job of organizing a spectacular funeral for him. David had Marat's body displayed at the Panthéon on a Roman bed with the knife wound visible and his right hand holding a pen – the 'weapon' of revolutionary journalism. Thousands of people came to see Marat's body. The only problem was, it had to be constantly sprayed with vinegar to suppress the horrific smell of the rotting corpse... Finally the smell became so bad, that Marat had to be urgently buried, ahead of the schedule... After the funeral David painted *The Death of Marat* – possibly his most famous painting – to confirm the role of Marat as the 'martyr' in the 'civil religion' of the revolution. Scholars believe that the violence that followed the death of Marat led to the Reign of Terror. With his work David knowingly contributed to cultivating rage among the radical revolutionaries.

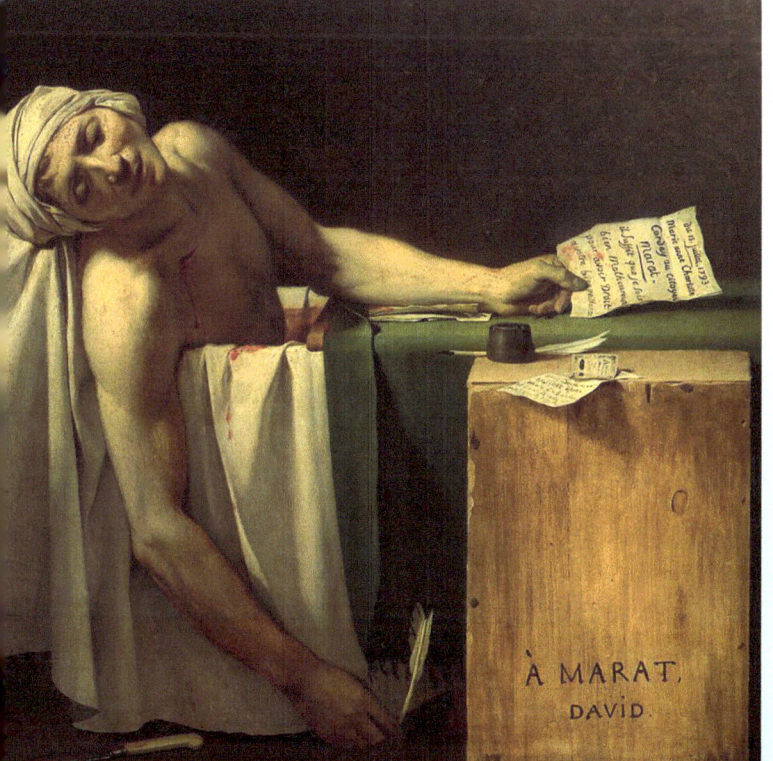

After Robespierre was arrested, David knew he was next. He pretended he had a 'stomach pain' and stopped attending the National Convention meetings. They still arrested him, but didn't execute. At his trial he shook with fear and mumbled promises, saying in the future he would stand for principles and truth rather than for this or that politician.

The judges let him go. And so the next chapter of David's life began. From the fanatical supporter of the French republic who sent hundreds of royalists to the guillotine, our artist transformed into the propaganda chief of an absolute monarchy – the Napoleonic empire. You can't make this up: David's royalist wife remarried him!

As Marat and other 'martyrs' of the revolution were tossed out of the Panthéon, and Napoleon's star was rising, David followed the future emperor begging to paint his portrait. Finally, in 1797, hoping to get rid of the artistic bootlicker, Napoleon agreed to be sketched. That was the only time he posed for a portrait by David. David created many portraits of Napoleon using that one sketch. Napoleon appreciated David's readiness to flatter and serve as a propaganda tool. He started giving him jobs – commissions for paintings that would glorify Napoleon's victories and his rise to power. David knew his place and didn't mind stretching and bending the truth when necessary. For example, when Napoleon commissioned David a painting of himself crossing the Alps mountains (*Napoleon at the Saint-Bernard Pass*), he asked to be portrayed on a horse, even though during the crossing he rode a mule. There was one embarrassing problem, however. During his term on the Committee of Public Safety, David signed the death sentence of a French general Alexandre de Beauharnais, whose widow, Josephine, became Napoleon's wife and empress... But David made himself so valuable to Napoleon, that his past was 'forgotten.'

Propaganda vs Truth: "Napoleon at St.Bernard Pass" by Jacques-Louis David (left) and by Paul Delaroche (right)

Napoleon used art to *legitimize* his rule (make it look *legitimate*, in keeping with the laws and expectations of society). The many artists who worked for him, including David, created what became known as the **Empire Style**. The Empire style made a visual connection between Napoleon's rule and the rule of the emperors of ancient Rome. Fashion, architecture, furniture design – everything had an

An 1814 French caricature: "A creator of historical paintings encouraged by the government" makes fun of David serving his new master, Napoleon

'ancient Roman' look, and Roman military and state symbols – eagles, palm leaves, and laurel wreaths appeared everywhere. Table and chair legs looked like winged lions and sphinxes. Images from Roman art and mythology – the **cornucopia** (the horn of plenty), lyres, bows and arrows, Venus and Mars – covered the walls and the clothes all across Europe.

In 1804, David became Napoleon's official court painter. He was much praised and had dozens of students. After the fall of Napoleon he left for Brussels where he died in 1825 hit by a carriage in a traffic accident.

Empire Style architecture: Triumphal Arch in Paris, built in 1806, imitated triumphal arches of ancient Rome. Left: examples of Empire Style design.

ADMIRAL NELSON
1758 – 1805
LADY HAMILTON
1765 – 1815

Admiral Nelson, a British Navy commander during the Napoleonic wars, was an unlikely character to make a spectacular career on the high seas. He had poor health, and, despite decades in the navy, suffered from sea sickness throughout his life. Yet his victories against Napoleon's fleet made him one of the greatest British military heroes.

Horacio Nelson was one of 11 kids born to a middle-class English family in Norfolk. When he was 12, Spain attacked the Falkland Islands, a British colony in the South Atlantic, and Horacio sailed off to war on the battleship of his uncle, who was a British Navy commander. The conflict ended in a peace treaty, but Nelson didn't want to go back home and attend school – he continued working as a common sailor for his uncle.

During the American Revolutionary War, in 1778, 20-year-old Horacio Nelson was given the command of a British ship. While chasing American and French vessels in the Caribbean, he became friends with local British colonists and married Frances (Fanny), daughter of a Caribbean sugar plantation owner. As a result Nelson formed a positive view of slavery – a fact that made him extremely unpopular among Enlightenment-inspired Europeans. He believed slavery was essential to the survival of the colonial economy, and that anti-slavery ideas were just a tool for manipulating public opinion, rather than any honest concern about the well-being of slaves.

Left: Nelson Column on Trafalgar Square in London

Returning to Europe, Nelson participated in operations against the Spanish, including ambushing and capturing Spanish ships carrying gold from the Americas. In 1797 Nelson came up with a plan to attack the town of Santa Cruz on the island of Tenerife of the Canary Islands to capture gold recently delivered there by a Spanish treasure ship. The Battle of Santa Cruz ended in a disaster for the British. The British assault troops landed in Santa Cruz, but by the time they fought their way to the main square, their boats had been burned by the Spanish, and they were trapped. They negotiated their way out and left empty-handed. Meanwhile, during the sea battle, Nelson's right arm was fractured by a musket ball and had to be amputated right

"Sir Horacio Nelson wounded at Teneriffe" by Richard Westall.

then and there. Half an hour after the amputation Nelson was back in action, giving orders to his captains. The defeat at Santa Cruz was quickly forgotten. The British public celebrated Nelson's courage and blamed the failure on the prime minister and his cabinet.

Nelson's wife Frances

Military fame came to Nelson at the Battle of the Nile in 1798. Napoleon landed in Egypt. From Egypt he intended to go to India to drive the British from there with the help of local rebels. He wanted his empire to link East and West. "Europe is but a molehill," he said. "All the great glories have come from Asia."
Nelson was ordered to prevent Napoleon's Indian campaign. As his fleet approached Alexandria, one of his captains asked him "If we succeed, what will the world say?" "There is no if," responded Nelson. "We shall succeed. Who may live to tell the story, is a very different question."

During the battle the British managed to surround the French navy and sink a number of French ships. The French flagship caught fire, and the gunpowder it carried blew up killing the crew and the French commander. The bay was coated in thick smoke for hours. During the 12-hour battle Nelson was hit in the forehead with a piece of explosion debris, and temporarily blinded. He exclaimed, "I'm killed..." and fell, but soon regained consciousness and refused to have his wound treated before the wounded among his crew were taken care of.

After the Battle of the Nile Nelson became a living legend. Monarchs of Europe sent him letters of admiration. He was given the title of Baron Nelson of the Nile and a pension of £2000 a year. The East India Company, that ran British colonies in India, made him a present of £10,000. From Alexandria Nelson's fleet sailed to Italy. The Queen of Naples, Maria Carolina, the sister of Marie Antoinette, greeted Nelson with these words: "O brave Nelson! What do we not owe you! O conqueror, savior of Italy! O God, bless and protect our brave deliverer!"
In Naples Nelson met the British ambassador, Sir William Hamilton, and his wife, Emma, Lady Hamilton, a close friend of Maria Carolina – and an admirer of Admiral Nelson.

"The Battle of the Nile" by George Arnald

Emma Hamilton was the child of a blacksmith. Her father died when she was a baby. She spent her childhood in poverty and started working as a maid at age 12. Some of her employers were London actresses who taught Emma dance and acting, and hired her to perform in theater productions. At some point she became the girlfriend of Charles Greville, a British politician and collector of antiquities, but he was not interested in marrying her. He wanted to find a wealthy bride to improve his financial situation, and eventually he found one. To get rid of Emma, he convinced his uncle, Lord Hamilton, to take her on a trip to Naples where Hamilton was appointed an ambassador. Greville lied to Emma, saying he would join them in a couple weeks. Emma left for Italy, and soon figured out that she was deceived and discarded. However, by that time, Lord Hamilton had fallen in love with her and proposed her marriage. Their marriage was quite happy until 7 years later, when Admiral Nelson arrived in Italy in 1798.

Soon after Nelson's arrival, Emma Hamilton invited 1800 guests to celebrate his 40th birthday. He had one arm, could see with only one eye, had lost most of his teeth, and suffered from violent fits of cough, but to Emma and her circle he was a great hero, and she did everything to charm him. Indeed, soon Nelson fell in love with her, and their relationship became known to Lord Hamilton and to Nelson's wife, Fanny. Lord Hamilton felt guilty that he had helped his nephew deceive and abandon Emma. He thought he didn't deserve her love, and tried to ignore the situation with Nelson, only hoping that gossipers wouldn't pay too much attention to it. But, of course, they did pay attention, and soon the story of Admiral Nelson and Lady Hamilton was in every English newspaper. Nelson's wife Fanny confronted her husband about this, but Nelson was harsh with her and sent her away. Emma Hamilton became a celebrity – the scandal of her relationship with Nelson kept them both in the news, and that's what they both wanted.

There was an even darker side to their relationship. The Queen of Naples Maria Carolina, dreaming of revenge following the death of her sister Marie Antoinette, wanted to convince her husband, the king, to declare war on France, but the king was – with good reason – afraid of Napoleon. The Queen asked Lady Hamilton for help, and Emma persuaded Nelson to advise the king that war against the French was a good idea. Soon the king's army was marching and – almost instantly – running back to Naples – defeated by the French. The royal family and the Hamiltons had to escape through an underground passage that led from the palace to the sea shore, where they were rescued by Nelson, who took them to Palermo on his ship, the Vanguard. For Naples it was a catastrophe. For Emma Hamilton – a romantic adventure.

Back in England, Nelson and Emma Hamilton felt pressured to live an extravagant, high-cost lifestyle to match the image they had created for themselves – that of wealth, fame, celebrity, and public admiration. In reality they never had enough money. Nelson borrowed money to buy a house so they could move in together. Emma and Nelson had a daughter, but kept secret the identity of the baby's father. When he traveled, performing his military duties, Emma suffered from loneliness, gave in to depression, and became a heavy drinker. A friend of the family wrote about her, "She is bold and unguarded in her manner, has grown fat, and drinks freely." She also started gambling, wasting enormous amounts of money.

"Admiral Nelson and Lady Hamilton"
by Herbert Gustave Schmalz

In 1805 Nelson won the greatest victory of his naval career – the Battle of Trafalgar against the joint French and Spanish fleet. 27 British ships, in two lines, a mile apart, approached 33 French and Spanish ships moving in a 5 miles-long formation off the coast of Spain, between Cadiz and Gibraltar, near Cape Trafalgar. Nelson directed his ship, the Victory, straight toward the enemy. Then he sat down and wrote his will and a prayer, asking God for victory. After that, signal flags were raised, messaging to the British fleet Nelson's famous words, "England expects that every man will do his duty."

"Nelson's last signal at Trafalgar" by Thomas Davidson

"Nelson at Trafalgar" by William Overend

Victory sailed into the battle at the head of the British fleet, and Nelson's officers advised him that as a commander he shouldn't expose himself to unnecessary danger. The captain of Victory asked Admiral Nelson to change his coat so that the enemy sharpshooters couldn't identify him by the glittery star-shaped military decorations he wore on his chest. Nelson replied: "In honor I gained them, in honor I shall die with them." He also refused to let other ships lead the attack.

As Victory came under fire, Nelson's assistant officer was instantly killed. Another one took his place and also perished minutes later along with 50 British fighters on Victory. Then Nelson was hit by a musket ball and fell down with the words, "They have done it at last..." Nelson's officers took him to his cabin, and gave him some wine to relieve his pain, but it was clear that his wound was fatal. "Give your services to those for whom there is some hope," Nelson told the ship doctor. "You can do nothing for me." Soon the captain of the Victory came to tell Nelson that 18 of the 33 enemy ships were surrendering. Nelson said goodbye to him and asked him to "take care of poor Lady Hamilton." His last words were recorded as "Thank God I have done my duty" and "God and my country."

Heard ye the thunder of battle
Low in the South and afar?
Saw ye the flash of the death-cloud
Crimson over Trafalgar?
Such another day never
England will look on again,
Where the battle fought was the hottest,
And the hero of heroes was slain!
("Trafalgar" by Francis Turner Palgrave, 1805)

Nelson's letter to Lady Hamilton

British king George III cried when he heard of Nelson's death. "We have lost more than we have gained," he said. Lady Hamilton was in grief for many weeks. Then it became known that in his will Nelson had left all his possessions to his son – except the house where he and Lady Hamilton lived. By that time Lord Hamilton had died, and Emma had no money to maintain her glamorous lifestyle. Yet, she couldn't let go of her spending habits, and continued to waste money. Soon she fell into debt and in 1811 she was put in a debtor's prison.

Then a scandal erupted. Despite Nelson's request that his letters to her be burned, Lady Hamilton kept them. In 1814 they were stolen and published under the title *Letters of Lord Nelson to Lady Hamilton*. The impression the letters gave was that Emma Hamilton broke Nelson's family and used him to become a celebrity. The last of Emma's friends abandoned her and the British public lost any sympathy for her. Later that year Lady Hamilton and her daughter escaped England for the French town of Calais where they rented a modest apartment. In addition to heavy drinking Emma started taking laudanum, a debilitating drug derived from opium. She died of alcoholism and drug abuse in 1815, at the age of 49.

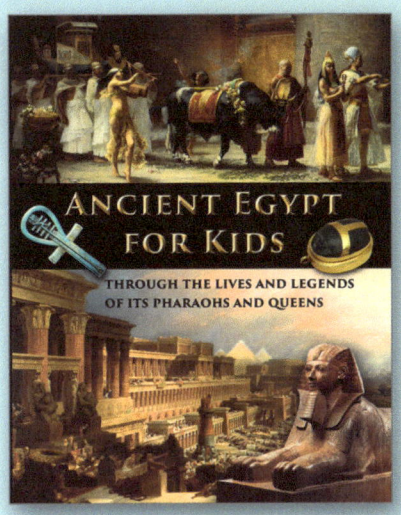
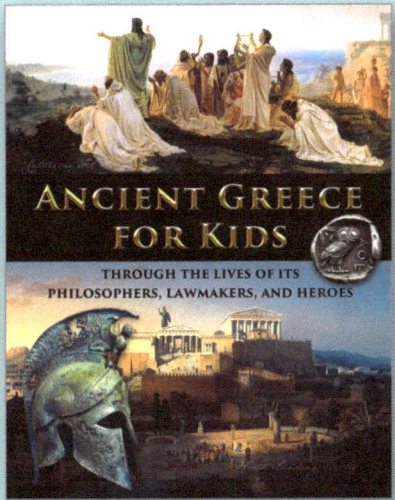
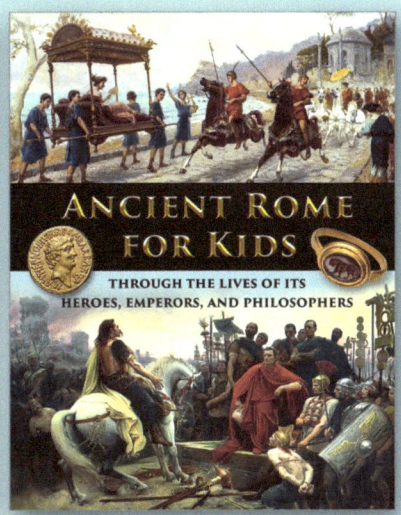
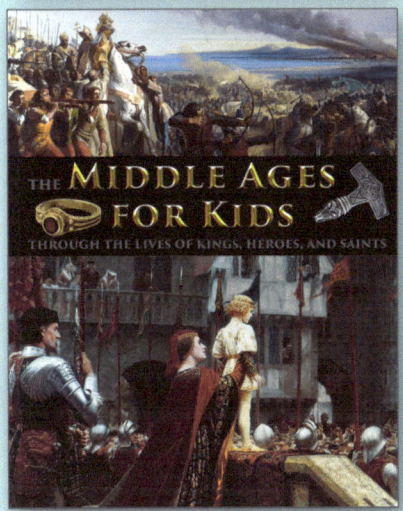
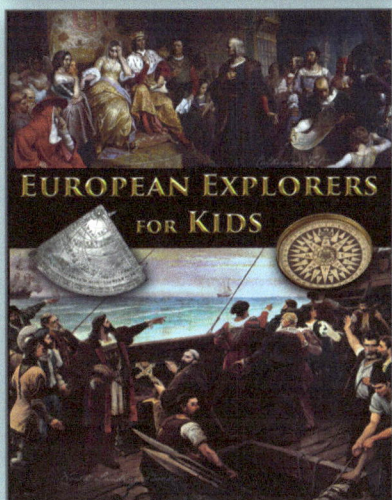
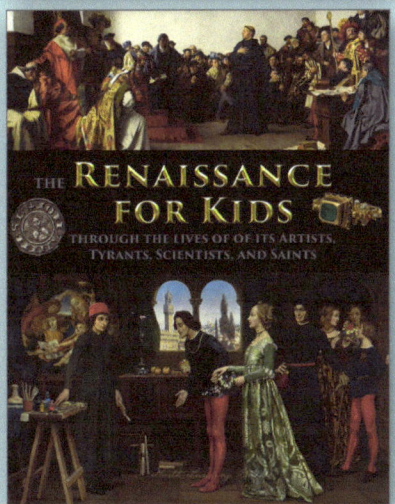
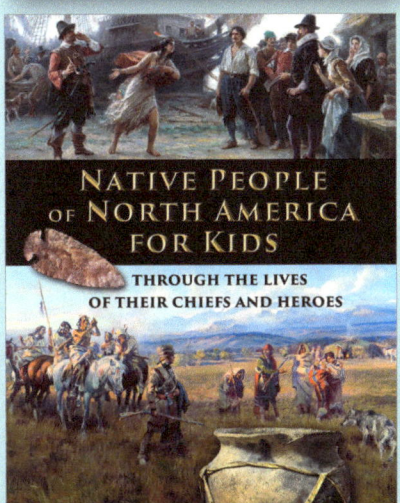
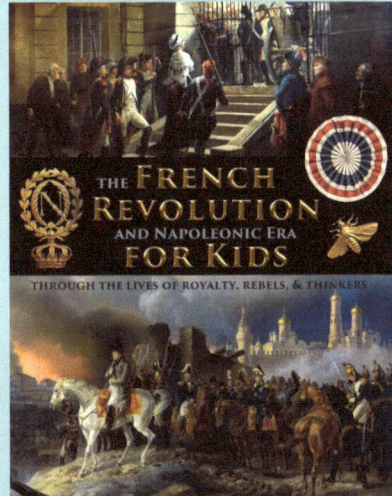
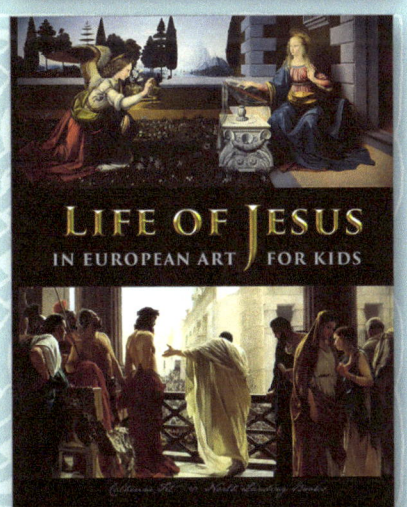

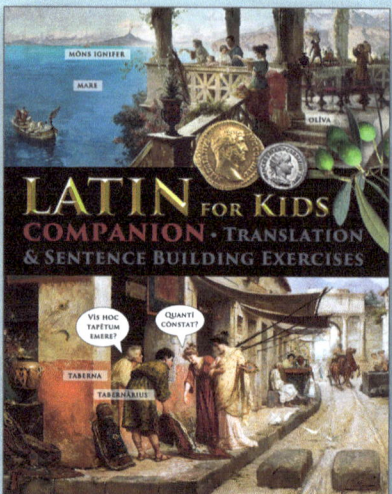

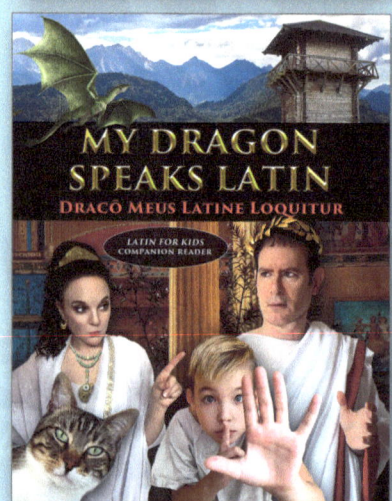
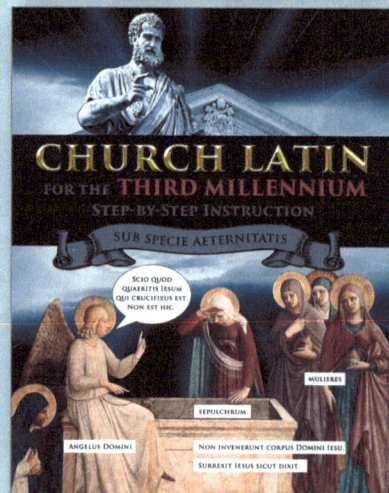
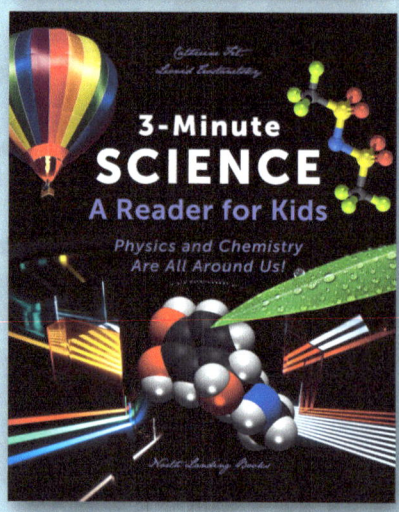
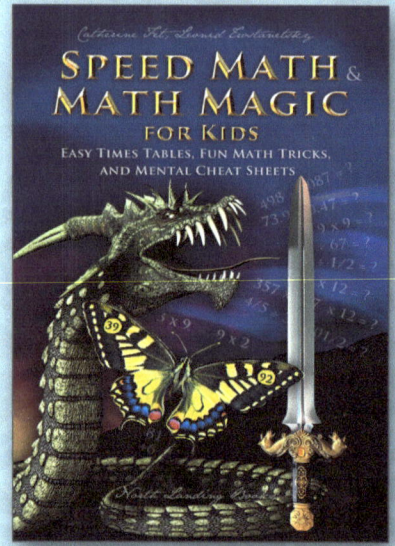
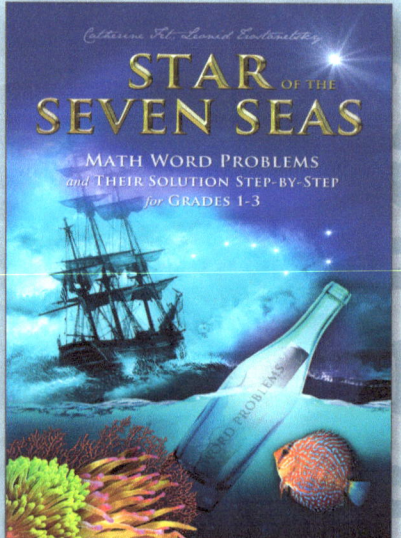

www.ingramcontent.com/pod-product-compliance
Lightning Source LLC
Chambersburg PA
CBHW041433010526
44118CB00002B/60